LINDA

McCULLOUGH

MOORE

THE BOOK OF

NOT

SO COMMON

PRAYER

A New Way to Pray, A New Way to Live

ABINGDON PRESS
NASHVILLE

THE BOOK OF NOT SO COMMON PRAYER
A NEW WAY TO PRAY, A NEW WAY TO LIVE

Copyright © 2014 by Linda McCullough Moore

Library of Congress Cataloging-in-Publication Data has been requested.

ISBN 978-1-4267-7833-9

Scripture quotations unless noted otherwise are from the Common English Bible. Copyright © 2011 by the Common English Bible. All rights reserved. Used by permission. www.CommonEnglishBible.com.

Scripture quotations marked "NKJV™" are taken from the New King James Version®. Copyright © 1982 by Thomas Nelson, Inc. Used by permission. All rights reserved.

Scripture quotations marked KJV are taken from The Authorized (King James) Version. Rights in the Authorized Version in the United Kingdom are vested in the Crown. Reproduced by permission of the Crown's patentee, Cambridge University Press.

Scripture quotations marked (NIV) are taken from the Holy Bible, New International Version®, NIV®. Copyright © 1973, 1978, 1984, 2011 by Biblica, Inc.™ Used by permission of Zondervan. All rights reserved worldwide. www.zondervan.com. The "NIV" and "New International Version" are trademarks registered in the United States Patent and Trademark Office by Biblica, Inc.™

Scripture quotations marked WEB are taken from the World English Bible.

14 15 16 17 18 19 20 21 22 23—10 9 8 7 6 5 4 3 2 1
MANUFACTURED IN THE UNITED STATES OF AMERICA

To Asa
Judd and Katie
Gideon and Joshua
and to their
children's children

*And behold, the L*ORD *passed by,*
and a great and strong wind tore into the mountains
*and broke the rocks in pieces before the L*ORD,
*but the L*ORD *was not in the wind;*
and after the wind an earthquake,
*but the L*ORD *was not in the earthquake;*
*and after the earthquake a fire, but the L*ORD *was not in the fire;*
and after the fire a still small voice.

—1 Kings 19:11-12 (NKJV)

CONTENTS

INTRODUCTION

A FEW YEARS AGO, SOMETHING HAPPENED to seriously rattle my cage—in fact, rattle it so absolutely that the cage door sprang open. I was attending a conference on spiritual disciplines, and I chanced to overhear a comment about a monk who lived centuries ago. That monk: Brother Lawrence.

I've always been a major fan of Brother Lawrence, who teaches in the book *The Practice of the Presence of God* that we can be in prayer all the time—while we are preparing food, teaching a class, or caring for a child. Brother Lawrence writes of a life of menial labor in the kitchen of his monastery, scrubbing pots and baking bread, all the while in fervent prayer and worship, reveling in the grace of God, in deep communion with his Savior, even as he worked. Seventeenth-century multitasking. The notion fit so nicely in my jam-packed, twenty-first-century life.

But that day at the conference, I learned that what gets left out of the story is that this same Brother Lawrence who practiced God's presence while working also participated in formal, liturgical, corporate prayer eight times a day. Eight times. Every day. *Then,* he prayed without ceasing. I always wondered why my experience of prayer was not more like the one he described. It's sort of like having been given a cake recipe that left out the part about turning on the oven. (And I always wondered why my cake was more like soup.)

Brother Lawrence had a discipline of prayer. Many times a day. Ah, I think, but that was then; this is now. Brother Lawrence didn't have a carpool, children, e-mails, committees, jobs, and a cell phone. *But,* he did have a soul and a Savior, just the same as I. And he did have a moment-to-moment relationship with God in Christ that my heart often longs for, an intimacy of constant and soulful connection.

So. The conference ends. I go back home, bring in the mail, wash up the dishes that did not wash themselves while I was away, and I begin to wonder. What if I tried this? What if I tried to pray, not eight, but maybe four times a day? For fifteen minutes, say. I, whose discipline for physical exercise involves two friends coming to my house to drag me physically to the gym. I, who can sit down for a minute to watch the evening news and rise to standing an entire two-hour, twelve-commercial movie later.

Brother Lawrence's formal practice of praying several times each day was so very different from anything in my experience. I, who actually believe that prayer might be the most important thing in life, had to admit I prayed when it was convenient. I loved God. I wanted to know him, and I gave prayer about five minutes a day. And even then, I might skip praying if the alarm clock failed or someone called a meeting before 9 a.m.

But it was as though I had been told a precious secret, and I remember the excitement I first felt when I decided I would try it. I would pray four times a day. And from the very start, and through the years that followed, the practice of praying in this way has been transformative. Spending time with God every few hours means God is on my mind; I'm conscious of his love as I move through the day; I see things through his eyes. This is no state of perfection. In fact, I am far more aware of my failings and my sin, which means I am continually awestruck at the cost Christ paid to bring us, every one, to a state of grace. This new practice has become a lovely swirl of holy consciousness, repentance, gratitude, and substantive blessing.

This new practice has become a lovely swirl of holy consciousness, repentance, gratitude, and substantive blessing.

In this book I will share my journey, step by step, as I moved—sometimes smoothly, sometimes by fits and starts—to a new way to pray, a new way to live. This will be a conversation, an exploration of the meaning and the practice of this thing called prayer, and it will be a guidebook, offering nuts-and-bolts, practical help to get from here to there, from longing and dissatisfaction to a daily, hourly practice of heart-blessing, life-changing, not-at-all-common prayer.

But, with God's help, it is prayer that *can be* common for us all.

We know that it is possible to read a hundred books on prayer and still not pray. But it is my hope—and yes, my oft-prayed prayer—that this book will help you to discover why that is the case and what might be the remedy. I pray this book will not only help you learn *about* prayer but indeed will also help you come to pray.

We who are disciples of God, in Christ, by the power of the Holy Spirit, share one sneaky suspicion, which is that prayer may be the pathway to the meeting of our needs, needs we may hide well—even from ourselves—but needs that define who we are and how we live. In our quiet moments, when we stop long enough to realize those vague feelings that something might be missing in our lives, we suspect that *something* might be God. And yet, we do not pray. Or if we do, we do not pray as we might, as we suspect in our heart of hearts that we are meant to pray. But—and this is one gigantic *but*—God is faithful. It is his pleasure to draw our hearts to him. He does not bless us based upon our efforts, but based entirely on who and what he is. It is God who enables us to conform to his design for us. And, without any doubt, we are designed to pray.

In that spirit, in *the* Spirit, I offer you here a bit of help along the way, and may you then help others, as we use our lives to pray.

Chapter One

ONE PILGRIM'S STORY

IMAGINE A PERSON WHO FOR YEARS and years has grabbed coffee and a bagel each morning and then fasted till the next day, taking only sips of water, juice, or soda maybe, grabbing a cracker or a pretzel when her busy life made that a thing that she could easily do. And then, imagine one day she hears of this new approach to nourishment. Something called *meals*. Three times a day. Cereal with milk and coffee in the morning; entire sandwiches at lunchtime; meat, pasta, salad, and crusty bread for dinner; and at bedtime, a piece of apple pie like you haven't tasted since you were a child. That comparison comes closest to describing the change in my life once I started praying for fifteen minutes four times a day. It gave a whole new meaning to the instruction to "taste and see how good the LORD is" (Psalm 34:8).

With prayers spaced throughout the day, I was never far away from prayer, and it was never a long journey to return. I found myself anticipating the sweetness of my times with God, looking forward to the resting or to the intensity of deep-heart conversing that my former prayers never allowed time for. And yes, of course, I found myself thinking: *My, aren't I holy, praying all the time.* But frequent prayers make sin stand out in stark relief, and instant cries for forgiveness and mercy run throughout my day.

I might have expected that when I began this new discipline it would be like pulling teeth—that difficult and painful. But prayer is what we were made for; prayer is a spiritual connection with the Living God. It is not an ordinary experience.

Prayer is what we were made for, prayer is a spiritual connection with the Living God.

Once I had completed the daunting task of upending my life to take on this new challenge, I found that it was like coming home to a place I had only dreamed about. We are creatures designed by God to operate in a certain way. When we are in harmony with our design, we function well, and when we are out of harmony with our design, we don't. A whale stranded on a beach flops about. Ah, but see him in the water and he is the magnificent creature God made him to be. And when we are in communion with our Lord in prayer, we are something to behold—something God beholds with pleasure.

Don't get me wrong. I am not saying that the change from snatching snacks to sitting down to three meals a day was a slight thing. It was enormous. It called for a radical overhaul of my weekly schedule, an upset of priorities and commitments, a rearranging of relationships and, especially, of my mind-set. It meant revision of my goals. And the preparation took more thought and energy and planning than the prayer. Think about preparing a Thanksgiving dinner. It takes ten hours to make the meal, and one hour to eat it. Or, consider the preparation for painting a room, the taping and moving furniture and covering everything in sight, all of it requiring much more time than the actual brushstrokes.

The first thing I had to do was take a look at how I spent my time, and then ask about every activity on the list: *Is it necessary or optional?* And then the next question: *Can I reduce the amount of time I spend on this? Can I make do with sleeping ten fewer minutes? Can food preparation time be cut?* When Martha raised that question with Jesus, he had some pretty specific thoughts on the subject (Luke 10:41). *Do I need to open junk mail, answer every e-mail and every cell phone call, shop, read magazines, and watch the news?*

If you own a full apartment building and you want to move in a new tenant, you must first evict one tenant who is already living there. We don't have blocks of time sitting vacant, waiting to be filled with prayer. They are already filled with other activities that we will no longer be able to do. To give prayer a central place in my life, I had to eliminate a number of things that felt pretty vital to me—or rather, they felt vital until I tried prayer in their place.

Until praying became routine, I literally wrote my prayer times in my calendar. I decided for the sake of practicality that I would not stick to set times, although I do love the grounding, reverent aspect of the formal honoring of God at set times of worship through the day. Instead, I made my daily prayer times first thing in the morning, right before (or some days instead of) lunch, then at the end of the afternoon, and finally, late in the evening—but I allowed myself flexibility so that "first thing in the morning" meant 6:30 some days and 8:30 others.

My experience of praying became enlivening and regular—that is, until it waned. I found that regular prayer is not an easy course to chart. I am very good at falling by the wayside, but just because I failed and had to begin again—and again—does not mean that I do not believe this is the way of prayer that I want in my life.

New Times, New Prayers

As I began my new practice, it became clear pretty quickly that not only when but *how* I prayed was also going to change. For too long, prayer had often been my sitting with my head bowed and my eyes closed, asking God to bless me and my dear ones, asking a quick blessing on the day, and hurrying away. So, I began to acquire several collections of prayers written by saints down through the ages—some prayers prayed a thousand years ago—prayers I prayed with concentration and intent.

And I began praying Scripture (and not just the Psalms), reading each word very slowly, forming each phrase into a prayer. This was very different from my *study* of Scripture. Now the Scripture studied me.

Prayer is being consciously in God's presence, focusing our eyes on him, on who he is, on what he's like. My prayer took the form of singing hymns and songs of praise, sitting, kneeling, standing, hands raised high, or falling on my face before God. We are flesh and blood. We must pray with our bodies. My prayer was also contemplation, meditation, listening to God's voice, sometimes writing letters to God, even e-mails. Often for evening prayers I would light a candle, sometimes with Gregorian chant playing softly—the candle and the chant helping to focus my thoughts on him—standing in my often-chilly kitchen late at night, praying to the One who is the light of the world.

We are flesh and blood. We must pray with our bodies.

My prayer might find me standing all alone in the middle of a deserted ball field on a clear winter's day, singing out in that beautiful air "Crown Him with Many Crowns." I walk a lot, and I've often stopped to praise the sunset. I began stopping to praise the sun setter. The sun riser. The already risen Son of God. I have a particular spot on a worn and wobbly bench in a local park that is my prayer place there. I have a corner in my sunroom where I sit, being consciously in the presence of God, sitting down alone in the evening, leaning on him, and talking the whole thing over, filling my mind with images of him. Prayer became astonishing. I began living into the discovery that prayer is the most outrageous, enlivening thing that we can do.

The Hours of Prayer in Scripture— and in Our Modern Lives

Throughout the Gospels Jesus is always going off to be alone with his Father. He would leave *in the middle of something (!)* to go pray. Jesus needed that. His heart longed for that. Jesus often withdrew to pray (Luke 5:16), going up into the hills by himself, being with his Father there (Matthew 14:23).

And throughout the Bible, there are set times for prayer, specifically the third hour, the sixth hour, and the ninth hour of the day—or 9:00 a.m., 12 noon, and 3:00 p.m.—prayer times observed by the Old Testament saints, the New Testament church, *and* our Lord Jesus Christ.

Three times a day Daniel prayed (Daniel 6:10). And in the Book of Acts, it was the *third hour* on the day of Pentecost when 120 disciples were in the upper room praying and were filled with the Holy Spirit (Acts 2:3, 15). The New Testament church customarily went to the temple at the hours of prayer. "Peter and John went up together into the temple at the hour of prayer, being the *ninth hour*" (Acts 3:1 KJV, emphasis mine). And Cornelius was in prayer at about the *ninth hour* when an angel of the Lord appeared to him in a vision, and Peter went up on the housetop to pray at about the *sixth hour* when he saw a vision of a great sheet, full of all kinds of beasts, let down from heaven (Acts 10:9).

Jesus was crucified in the *third hour* of the day (Mark 15:25). The darkness at noonday occurred in the *sixth hour* (Mark 15:33; Matthew 27:45). Finally, at the time of the evening prayer, the *ninth hour*, Jesus gave up the ghost (Luke 23:44). These hours of prayer are memorials of him who made it possible for us to come boldly before the throne of God in prayer (Hebrews 10:19).

And yet we say: We don't have time to pray. We imagine that we are the first to have demanding lives. We think that we invented *busy*. But *busyness* has always been. Martin Luther said he generally prayed two hours every day, except on very busy days. On those days, he prayed three. Luther was the dictionary definition of a busy man—defending theology, translating the Bible, writing, leading a Reformation, not to mention tending hearth and home. Family and children, the care of others' lives, the most relentless occupation of them all. Susannah Wesley, mother of John and Charles, gave birth to nineteen children, of whom ten lived to adulthood. This home-schooling mom prayed two hours every day, and when there wasn't solitude to pray, she would sit down in a corner and flip her apron up over her head. Her children knew that meant that she was in communion with the very God. Hudson Taylor, that missionary to China who changed the world, lived days far, far too busy to pray, and so he rose at 2 a.m. and prayed till 4 a.m.

How do we get from where we are to this new way of being? How do we arrive at that place of continuous connection, unbroken fellowship, where every breath breathes in his love, breathes out his majesty?

Not by dropping by for a quick "Dear God," a fast "Thank you for this day. Please bless me on my way. I see our time is up."

"Well, it's a start," we say.

But I have come to think this may not be the case. Perhaps it's not a start at all but rather an ironclad guaranteed finish, for the simple reason that it is, by design, as doomed to failure as is devoting five minutes a day to any enterprise we deeply value.

"I tried." "I prayed." "Nothing much happened." "I gave it a shot."

I think the devil must dearly love short prayers, the quick and easy kind where we can dip one toe in, tell ourselves we did it, and console each other: "Prayer is hard." We shake our heads and say, "It's not easy," as if to say God isn't always there, when truth be told, we haven't stuck around long enough to find out whether he is or not. We knock on the gates of heaven, then scribble a quick note we stick between the rails, and run back to our busy lives. "I guess nobody's home," we say.

"But it's not practical," says the voice of real life. "Not with the busyness of modern life."

But practical is precisely what it is.

It's how we work. It's how the world works. We are a civilization built upon the timed and timely foundation of our hour building blocks, cemented with the understanding that time is what's required to do a thing.

A soccer game takes ninety minutes, no matter how rushed a mother's day might be. A sitcom (with commercials) ties up the airwaves for thirty minutes—not twenty-nine, not thirty-one. A job demands forty hours every week, if we're lucky.

We may curse the frantic busyness of the lives we've chosen, but nonetheless, even given this, not one of us will rush into work tomorrow morning and announce, "I can only give this job two hours, tops, today," or hurry to the barbershop, the dentist's office, or a movie theater with a "Sorry, but I've got about ten minutes here to spare."

The magic word is *spare*.

We pray in such time as we have to spare.

Which is fine. We can do that. We can do whatever we want.

We can give God five or ten minutes, bending on one knee, one eye on the clock, the motor running.

We can even tell each other and ourselves that it is reasonable.

But let us not pretend our spirits and our God require no more. We need hours—one a day and sometimes more—to spend in mystical communion with the God of the universe, the Creator, our Father and our Lord.

"But who has an hour?"

We all do.

We all have twenty-four.

The reason we do not spend one of those hours every day in prayer is because we do not want to, and we do not want to because we have not spent an hour there.

"But what would I do for one whole hour?" The very thought is alarming.

Ah, but now that's the easy part.

You pray this prayer: "Our Father who art in heaven," the whole way through to "the kingdom, and the power, and the glory," but leave out the last "amen." And then you pray, "Now my Father and my God, I want to sit in praise and wonder, read Psalms—out loud—sing hymns, and read the hundreds of stories about you in Scripture. And then I want to talk with you about my life, which is so very hard sometimes. And I want to sit and listen, to hear what you will say to me that no one has ever heard before. I want to dive into the mystery that is to be with you."

I want to sit and listen, to hear what you will say to me that no one has ever heard before. I want to dive into the mystery that is to be with you.

I have learned a tender truth in this practice of prayer. It is this: *When we please someone, we love him more.* I know it works the other way around, but I believe this is also true. When I come to God at my little prayer times throughout the day, I believe I please him, and thinking that I give him pleasure intensifies the intimacy with my Lord. When a child feels the pleasure of his father, he loves his father more. He is drawn closer. It's how it works.

There's nothing magic about the choice of fifteen minutes. Praying for any interval four times every day could turn a life upside down. And is prayer four times a day for everyone? I don't know. Nor do I know whether it is in fact even possible for everyone to carve out four prayer times a day. I really do believe some individuals' lives are too complicated and demanding. But, I also know that those individuals are rare. I'm hard-pressed to think if I know one such person.

If God is a maybe, or even just a good idea, then it makes sense to pray a little in the morning and whisper prayers here and there through the day. But, if God is God, and if *the* God is interested in being in communion with me, then the only thing that makes even a particle of sense is to pursue him 24/7, to drop everything to enjoy that sweet, delicious honor.

Even presenting ourselves with the prospect of such a radical prayer practice will pose questions wanting honest answers. I asked a friend what would stop her from trying to spend time alone with God at set times through the day. Her answer: "I would have to want to. I would have to think it was important—more important than any other thing."

Chapter Two
WHY PRAYER?

I've got a truism that I'm almost certain is actually true. Here it is: If there's a frequent refrain in the Bible, a word or theme that shows up over and again, chances are it's downright central. Or, more simply put: If anything is in the Bible more than twenty times, you can bet there is a reason for it being there.

For example, the Bible is chock-full of verses that proclaim our God is greater than all other gods, greater than kings and rulers.

Frankly, these verses never made sense to me.

I mean, why would the *Lord* of all creation, the *Ruler* of the heavens and the universe, *the* God, even bother to state anything so patently obvious? I don't say to the thumbtack on the table: "I am far above you. I'm wiser and stronger, more dexterous and agile, in short, a better human being." So why would God compare himself to gods made out of brass and terra cotta, or even mortal flesh?

I don't take on the thumbtack; there's no contest. Why would God take on a president or Queen Elizabeth?

But he does take on other "gods." He goes out of his way to say he outdoes "kings" and "rulers," and his Holy Word repeats it like it means something. But what might that meaning be?

I don't think God is comparing himself to actual flesh-and-blood prime ministers and presidents. Rather, it seems to me that he is taking on the real gods we worship, the gods we give our very selves to, the gods we live and die for. He's saying, "I matter more than even these."

Let me name the gods we worship, all the things in life we deify. Silly gods: hockey, buffalo wings, and YouTube; serious, staid gods: education, status, and security; secret gods: fraud and pornography; subtle deities: self-image, personal best, and winner; churchy gods: morality, self-righteousness, and pride; old-fashioned gods: sloth, lust, and greed.

These are not our incidentals, harmless pastimes; rather, they are the objects of our worship and self-sacrifice and dedication. If that seems extremely stated, we can do the math; run the numbers; calculate the time we give to all these things and then compare that with the time we spend with God. We can evaluate their relative importance in our lives quite simply, just by going without them for a month.

Or, another telling exercise: we might write down 8:00, 8:30, 9:00, 9:30, 10:00, and each half-hour through the day until bedtime, and for each time write down what we have done, and in the margin, write who was god of that half-hour. God is not God of our lives if he is not God of our half-hours.

Time is the thermometer, the indicator of priorities of the things we value. So too, time used differently can alter who and what will rule our days. There's a well-kept secret of time management that doesn't get much press. It's this: If every morning you take five minutes and jot down what you will do with each half-hour of your day, that one small practice will actually change the things you do with time.

Time is the thermometer, the indicator of priorities of the things we value. So too, time used differently can alter who and what will rule our days.

Time. It's the one thing every blessed one of us is given in exactly the same amount. Donald Trump has no more minutes in his hours than you've got in yours. Oprah Winfrey has just seven days in every week she lives. Barack Obama gets 365 days every year, and once every four years when he gets an extra day, you get one too.

Jesus tells us: "Where your treasure is, there your heart will be also" (Matthew 6:21). Where you put your minutes is very likely where you put your heart.

I believe that the first step in acknowledging God as our truest treasure is showing up to pray. Every day. Even if it's raining. Even if it's not. Even if you have a hundred other things to do. And here's the astonishing surprise: You start to like this daily prayer. You start to need it. You start to miss it when it isn't there. You start to love it. You begin to treasure your time alone with God. It becomes the best-tasting, most melodious, harmonious, exciting, satisfying part of your whole day. You crave it, you can't get enough.

And guess what else? You don't end up living in a cave somewhere. You don't get voted the Hermit Saint. People appear from the most unlikely places; your life gets richer with experiences and happenings, relationship and blessing. You seek first the kingdom of heaven and God's righteousness. You put your treasure where your heart is; you say, out loud, in a big, bold, outdoor voice: "I will have no other God before you. You are my God."

You come to God in prayer—and you would be very well advised to hold onto your hat.

How Can I Do It If I Don't Know What It Is?

And yet, what is prayer? That one short word is asked to cover a multitude of mysteries. Prayer is worship. Prayer is sitting down with God, abiding in his love, filling our minds with images of him. Prayer is being in the presence of the living God and being acutely aware of how unlikely and astonishing that is. Prayer is resting. Prayer is wrestling. Prayer is the most outrageous and transforming thing that we will ever do, but often we reduce it to a wave, a knee bend, and a *please* and *thank you*. Prayer is, most simply put, being consciously in the presence of

Prayer is the most outrageous and transforming thing that we will ever do.

God. In a very true sense, prayer is *being*, not *doing*. It is less an activity than a location. (It goes without saying that we are in God's presence all the time, but being aware of this reality is another story.)

And yet prayer is not all peaceful and serene. I have been considering starting a campaign to abolish the term "quiet time." True, we prepare our hearts to receive God by quieting ourselves—stillness really is the place where it all begins—but what pervades our prayer times is often anything but quiet. There will be moments that are holy, soft and gentle, but so many others that we will experience as monumental and imposing, riveting our full attention. And, it must be said, we are guaranteed there will be times when prayer is dull and vacant, parched and dry as dry can be. These times will be interspersed with encounters with God we find to be enlightening, shocking, and in the end life-changing.

Prayer involves every aspect of our being: thought and reason, emotion and desire. This conversation with our Heavenly Father will encompass all of life. And it will surely touch our deepest beings, joining in rich paradox happiness and sorrow, satisfaction and disappointment. Prayer knows how to hold the contradictions of our lives in one brilliant understanding.

"Come now, and let us reason together" are the words we read in Isaiah 1:18 (KJV). Prayer can be exactly this: reasoning together. We do it all day long, with ourselves and with the people in our lives. We may not give it this name, but we are always thinking and deciding, discussing and arguing about ideas. Reasoning is part of prayer. Prayer can be the questions we ask God, and when we allow ourselves to listen, it can be the questions God asks us. "Have you ever stopped to think about it this way?" asks the Holy Spirit. Faith is not a blind venture; it is based on serious thought and understanding. On reasoning. On reason.

For anyone—such as me, to take one random example—whose first experience of prayer was limited to asking God for things, there is much to learn. And that's the good news. The challenge of learning to pray can get me out of bed some mornings. Imagine how boring and lifeless would be any practice that was not dynamic, multifaceted, and richly textured.

Perhaps a useful starting place might be to think about what it is we *do* in prayer, to help us move toward an understanding of living in a state of being with our Heavenly Father. Many Christians know the acronym ACTS, which offers one good description of prayer: *A*doration, *C*onfession, *T*hanksgiving, and *S*upplication. The order of the letters recommends the sequence we might pray.

First, we *adore*. Think of the bride and groom standing at the altar on their wedding day. It's not hard to imagine a bit of adoring as the first order of business, the natural impulse, automatic and exactly right. So it is that we are made to love and adore our Savior. But, the argument arises, marriage is a human relationship, not the connection of

God and his child. True, it's not; but human love can help us know the nature of adoring, caring, and blessing, so long as we do not confuse comparison with definition. We cannot think of relationship with God without referencing our experiences in human love. And so we do compare, always with the understanding that it is the same and it is different, that the two are alike and unalike, one a shadow image and the other the real thing.

In this sequence of prayer, we start out by adoring, knowing adoration as a feeling we have for those we love the most. And is this automatic? It is not. Or, not in my experience. It's hardly an exaggeration to say that it took me *approximately forever* to reach the place where I even knew what adoration of God could be. It has truly been a long time coming. And how did I get there? I prayed. I asked God to give me love for him. I prayed the truth; I prayed the very words, "I do not love you. Would you give me love for you?" And he did. There is nothing we can do apart from him. We cannot even love him. But what a blessing to be given access to the experience of adoration.

I have found that hymns of praise foster my adoring best of all. The music primes my heart, allowing words to penetrate my consciousness, enlarge my loving. I hear, "Angels, help us to adore him, / Ye behold him face to face; / Sun and moon bow down before him; / Dwellers all in time and space," and I glimpse heaven—angels, planets, and images beyond my knowing.

Sometimes, art can be the way in. Every public library in the United States has books of Christian paintings. Steal an hour. Take one off the shelf and sit with holy images, allowing them to touch you. Let God surprise your heart in worship in the middle of the reading room.

Adoration is my favorite part of prayer, the part that now resembles no other aspect of my life, the part that doesn't leave me second-guessing or dissatisfied. Taking certain pleasure in something outside ourselves feels wonderful, and when that *something* is definitively perfect, there's no downside. When we worship and adore anything or anybody who is not God, we are always shushing hushed but niggling, slight misgivings about the object of our worship. It sort of takes the edge off. But when we worship God, we adore perfection.

The second part of the ACTS prayer is *confession*. Here, even more clearly, we experience ourselves to be entirely dependent upon the grace of God. We pray that the Holy Spirit will convict us of sin, in order that we can confess. I know no more frightening human condition than for a person to think he is just fine when that is not the case, to be unaware of danger, which, if recognized, could easily be avoided. A blindfolded man runs toward the cliff's edge, laughing, saying he is fine. In our deepest beings, we must pray that God will show us the reality about ourselves, how fecklessly *we* run to peril.

I have a very simple exercise I do. It is modeled on the Daily Examen of Ignatius Loyola, which is a practice of prayerful reflection on the day in order to see God's presence and discover his direction. In the evening, I sit in a quiet place with my eyes closed, and I review the events of the day. It is almost like watching a movie as I bring all of the day's activities and interactions to mind. I watch this movie twice—the first time, on the lookout for all the ways I see God's hand in what has happened; the second time, praying to see the instances of things I've thought, and said, and done that have not been pleasing to the Lord. The Holy Spirit brings to mind those things for which I need to ask forgiveness.

Confession seems to be a focus on the negative, for so sin surely is, but paradoxically, this is the path to peace. There is nothing lovelier in all the world than to feel regret and pain for something I have done and then have God obliterate all memory of that forgiven sin. Sins, fire-engine red, washed freshly-fallen-snow bright white. We misunderstand the Cross if we think Christ died to mute remembrance.

The *T* in ACTS, *thanksgiving,* is perhaps a bit more straightforward. The primary glitch in this regard is trying to give thanks in the middle of the muddle of our lives. On a bright sunny day with no work and everybody healthy, our thanks is at the ready. But give us stormy weather, deep-sorrow sadness, or pain in mind or body, and praise is sometimes hard to come by. I have discovered, though, that it is an extraordinary experience in the middle of a migraine to sing out hymns of thankfulness. The blessing in those moments is the miracle that as I sing my heart fills up with what is good, and pure, and peaceful. I might still have the pain, but it is not the only thing contained in that one moment. I often wonder if I would know God as I do if I didn't have a migraine brain. Chronic, quirky, unpredictable, and disorienting migraines help keep me tethered to the Lord. I thank God for the agency of anything in life that draws me close to him.

Chronic, quirky, unpredictable, and disorienting migraines help keep me tethered to the Lord. I thank God for the agency of anything in life that draws me close to him.

If we wait for everything around us to be OK before we open up our hearts to praise, we will wait forever. The secret in life is to make a place for joy and thanksgiving no matter what the circumstance. "But that's impossible," you say. Of course it is. God traffics in the *impossible* all day. And if we are his children, so will we. Imagine a world where only the possible was possible. I wouldn't want to live there.

Our ACTS prayer ends with *supplication*, an antique word that is our invitation to ask God's blessing—for so very long, the first (and sometimes only) part in all my prayers. This aspect requires little explanation, except perhaps to say that there is nothing in the world we cannot ask God for. He is the One who says, "The very hairs of your head are all numbered" (Matthew 10:30 KJV). It is his will and pleasure that we come to him with every longing that there is. There is no part of daily life that we are not meant to bring to God in prayer.

I have a friend who has enlarged my thinking about prayers of supplication. This is a woman who has lived through a campaign of genocide, of ethnic cleansing, and she tells me she doesn't want to ask God for anything that she can get from any other source—she's thinking food, water, safety from being harmed—because she says if she gets that thing from some source other than God, then she will be inclined to worship that. She tells me she wants from God what one can get only from God. Me too. Basically. Only I don't know what that is or how to ask for it. But I love the way her words have made me think about my prayers of petition. There's the old saw: be careful what you ask for, you may get it. I thank God that he protects us from so many of our prayers, that he spares us by denying our requests. But it seems to me that my friend prays a holy prayer, one that will not be denied.

Gazing on God

ACTS is just one way of describing what prayer might be. Indeed, much of what we say *about* prayer, and certainly any comparisons we make between our conversations with God and our conversations with other people, will be no more than skimpy and segmented efforts to teach our hearts the truth. We know these little metaphors miss the supernatural mark, no doubt by several light years. And so, it is important that we square these comparisons with our theology, making sure they don't mislead us, cause us to invent some different deity. Do I overstate here? I don't think so. I know that personally I go through life inventing images of God and prayer that bear only slight resemblance to reality. I compare prayer to some ordinary chat, and so reduce it to a miniature approximation of the splendor that it is. And when I do this, I diminish prayer and chip God down to size as well. We must give thought to the comparisons we make. We must be careful what we say, for we are listening.

For example, prayer can surely be companionship, but it is not always like two friends meeting for coffee. More often, it is like one friend giving the other a blood transfusion; one giving the other life, physically and spiritually. I've said it before, and we all need to say it again—many times—prayer is a relationship between two beings, where one of the two is God, and one is not. Embedding prayer in Scripture will keep this at the forefront of our minds.

Prayer is so much more than our speaking words to God. It is God's communicating with us, working on us, transforming us into the image of God, making us more and more like him. Prayer is a workshop where we are handcrafted, completed, caused to be what we were designed and—by God's grace—created to be. For good or ill, whether we pray or not, we are always being changed; worked on by our surroundings; shaped and molded and defined. We get to choose the influences that will work upon us, but we do not get to choose their effect. In prayer we choose the influence of the Holy Spirit of the living God, never knowing what results might follow, but all the while trusting the One who says, "I know the plans I have in mind for you . . . ; they are plans for peace, . . . to give you a future filled with hope" (Jeremiah 29:11).

The outcome will not be our doing, but we know the One who will cause us to be more than we can ask or imagine. Our thoughts run to new hairstyles; his thoughts run to new heads, new thoughts, new perspectives, and brand-new understanding. Our thoughts run to fit bodies; his thoughts run to fit souls. We envision happy days; he envisions everlasting glory.

The focus of our prayers must be, with concentrated gaze, on God—because this focus is the only way to avoid making our prayers be for *our* glory. Even in our prayers for good things—for righteousness, for holiness—if we focus on ourselves and not on God, we'll lose our way for sure. I say that what I want is God, to live for him and in his glory, but sometimes I think what I really want is my *self*—but my self made perfect, in fact made wonderful, so I can feel really good about me, and who I am, and what I do. That is so very unlike a preference for the Lord himself. It is a subtle temptation; but even mechanical reminders to look at him, to "taste and see how good the LORD is" (Psalm 34:8), can help us redirect our gaze.

When we focus on ourselves, prayer can summon up both anxiety and worry. A time of quietness can set the stage for every shaky feeling there can be. *Worry as worship.* Make no mistake, we do know how to worship; the question is, *What is the object of the honor and attention that we give?* When I'm supposed to be adoring God, I catch myself fretting because I took a world-class lasagna to the Alpha class last night at church, and no one said how wonderful I was. I am worshiping. I am adoring the image of myself. I worry about my kids. I worship, I adore, a perfect family. I sit to pray and feel an old familiar twang of pain. I'm worried about my shoulder or my knee. I am worshiping my health.

"But shouldn't we adore health?" comes the question. Well, Paul prayed for healing, and God offered him grace instead (2 Corinthians 12:8-9). God got it right, or he got it wrong. We must decide. This is the magnitude of the questions we explore every time we pray. I want to say that prayer is not for the fainthearted, but of course prayer is precisely for the very faintest-hearted. We have only to be willing to leave our fright and fearfulness with God when we rise up from our knees. But far too often we pray, "Dear God, I'm worried and afraid. Please take these fears from me. In Jesus' name, Amen," and then we snatch them back before we walk away.

We can trade in times of gentle sweet communion, walking with God in the cool of the evening in the garden of Eden, for our frantic, harried pleas that God do what we say. There is a great line in the movie *Shadowlands*, a line I'm told may have been written specially for the movie. No

"Thy will be done" (Matthew 6:10 KJV). This prayer does not need to be cut to fit us; we need to be changed, transformed through the slow-drip splendor of God's grace, in order that we fit this prayer.

matter; it rings true. In the film the actor who plays C. S. Lewis says, "I do not pray because it changes God; I pray because it changes me." That is, we pray in order to be brought into conformity with the Lord's design. "Thy will be done," the smartest line in every prayer we pray. We have only to look back across the years and see the things we prayed for that would have been disastrous had our prayers been granted. Only after the passage of time can we see the answers that at the time seemed wrong but that have turned out to be for our solid, certifiable good. "Thy will be done" (Matthew 6:10 KJV). This prayer does not need to be cut to fit us; we need to be changed, transformed through the slow-drip splendor of God's grace, in order that *we* fit this prayer. But we start where we are. We walk before we run.

Prayer Is Connection in Community

Despite the fact that our conversation here is focused on private prayer, it is also true that we must always pray with others, and that the people in our lives will pervade our prayer times. Prayer is a way we are related, interconnected, dependent on and involved with others. In the Bible, we read the words of the prophet Samuel: "I would never sin against the LORD by failing to pray for you" (1 Samuel 12:23). No casual calling, this. The Trinity, the Three Persons, is a community, and so is the body of Christ. We are taught that we are members of one another—as deeply connected as that. We are to pray for and with each other always.

I sometimes wonder what somebody means when they say they'll pray for me, but with certain saints, I know exactly. When I ask my pastor for her prayers, I know she falls down on her knees and seeks God's mercy in fervent devotion. I also came to know what the man sometimes called "the evangelical pope" meant by praying for another. That man, John Stott, spoke one night at Amherst College. At the end of the evening, a long line formed to speak with him. I joined the line, and when my turn came, I spoke from a deep experience of the phrase "to covet someone's prayers." I said, "I'm here with my friend Annie. She does not know the Lord. Tonight when you are traveling over the Atlantic Ocean flying back home, would you please pray for Annie?"

John Stott looked at me with kindest eyes, and he said no.

"I will, however," he said, "pray for your friend right now," and as he stood there, surrounded, in a crowded auditorium of people who seemed unwilling to leave, he prayed a prayer that I will always remember. When John Stott prayed that night, I knew that I was praying with a man who walked with God. It was a prayer like few I have experienced in my life.

For saints, prayer comes first. It just does. It is the bedrock foundation of every action of every day. We are helped in prayer just knowing others pray. There is such beauty in awareness that when we pray the hourly prayers of the church, numberless others all across the world join hearts and minds together in that prayer.

Prayer connects us with other people when no other contact is possible. My ninety-seven-year-old aunt—the dictionary definition of a prayer warrior—never leaves her nursing home. But oh, the places she will go; oh, the places she has been. She's on more speed dials than anyone I know. "Will you pray?" Those three words have echoed down the years, and will be said with no less fervor in a call she might well get this afternoon. Her life is actively involved with people and events across the globe.

Prayer is praying for the people we love. Prayer is a dynamic, powerful, supernatural involvement with other people. Prayer might be asking God to bless a stranger on the street, the mail carrier, the librarian, your doctor, or the crossing guard. Prayer might be choosing one person, a close friend, or maybe someone you don't know particularly well and praying for him every single day, perhaps for years. You might be the only person who ever prayed for him. I had known and prayed for someone for twenty years who one day said to me, "I don't know if your beliefs in God are right or wrong, but you may be the only person on earth who cares about my soul." I repeat these words here because it is a calling every single one of us can take upon ourselves: to care, in prayer, for the soul of another.

There is another way, however, that we sometimes do damage to one another's prayer lives. Friends sigh and say to us, "You know, I hardly ever pray." And we commiserate and say, "I know. You're so busy now. It's so hard." And we sell each other down the river. We diminish these friends; we patronize and sell them short. In an effort to be nice—the scourge of humankind, I sometimes think—we fail to hold each other to account. Bottom line, we have to decide whether prayer is a harmless pastime, a lovely interlude, there to indulge in when we have the time, *or*, if it is food for body, soul, and mind, air to lungs, fire to life. If we decide prayer matters, we deprive and dishonor one another by placating, patting one another on the head, and saying it's OK not to pray. I can remember with precision those times in my life when I've said to a good friend, "I shouldn't do that," and the friend has replied, "No, you shouldn't." Replies like this can make us understand what friendship is. The Bible tells us to "consider one another to provoke unto love and to good works" (Hebrews 10:24 KJV).

May prayer itself be love and a good work.

Chapter Three
PRAYING TIME

I N MY OWN PRACTICE, PRAYING FIRST THING in the morning is the easiest of scheduled times for me, although it must be said that often God comes after the *New York Times* headlines, two cups of strong black tea, Facebook, and e-mails. I tell myself this order of the day finds me more awake by the time I get to prayer, but honesty demands that I admit it often finds me more distracted. Writers are often advised to write before any input of the day intrudes, and similarly I believe we would do well to pray first thing. These daily practices of ours do introduce us to our addictions, those (perhaps) harmless activities that we always put first. Am I more interested in who sent me an e-mail than I am in sitting down in communion with the God of all creation? My behavior would say yes. I am happy to praise Jesus for his matchless love, but first I must read the news on Facebook that a friend has finally decided to try going gluten-free. I find that once settled down to prayer in the morning, an hour passes quickly as I read and pray God's Word, sit and talk to God, and ideally, at some point cease the talking and begin to listen. My later prayer times through the day can meet with major problems of consistency as well as big-time lacking in the attentiveness department. I find distraction gains strength as the day progresses. The primary problem with midday is that it is midday. It's not only in the middle of the hours but also smack-dab in the center of the hopes I have to turn the day to some account. I find it most helpful then to go outside to pray, to stand and worship in the middle of my backyard or in some open space, wherever the day might find me.

Late afternoon finds energy at low ebb, and so these are the times when rousing music leads to worship that is restorative and heartfelt. I play praise songs, such as "Our God Is an Awesome God" or "These Are the Days of Elijah," and old stalwart hymns, such as "There Is Power in the Blood" or "Jesus Christ Is Risen Today," reminding me that every day is a new Easter in my heart. YouTube turns out to be a repository of glorious anthems to our God.

Evening seems to be the time for meditation: music now is soft and reverent; prayers are quiet, as is where I stand. I read the prayers of the church at the close of the day, always being reminded of life's endings— of the day, of our lives, and one day, of the fallen world.

From *The Book of Common Prayer*, I love these ancient prayers at close of day:

A day blessed by the righteousness and rhythms of divine communion is a balanced, precious thing.

Keep watch, dear Lord, with those who work, or watch, or weep this night, and give your angels charge over those who sleep. Tend the sick, Lord Christ; give rest to the weary, bless the dying, soothe the suffering, pity the afflicted, shield the joyous; and all for your love's sake.

Support us, Lord, all the day long, until the shadows lengthen, and the evening comes, the busy world is hushed, the fever of life is over, and our work done; then Lord, in your mercy, give us safe lodging, a holy rest and peace at the last.

A day blessed by the righteousness and rhythms of divine communion is a balanced, precious thing, freighted with the weight of glory, full of purpose, order, and a peace-filled grace.

Timing Is Everything

Your day of prayer may look very similar to mine, or very different. There are no hard-and-fast rules regarding the precise times of our daily prayers, but it will surely be worthwhile to give some consideration to scheduling. In this, as in every aspect of our daily practice, we will be more likely to continue if it is well-suited to our individual ways of being. What works very well for one person may work just as poorly for another.

As we begin to consider new ways of giving prayer a more central place in our daily lives, it might be most useful to consciously observe ourselves in action for a few days. Are we people of the clock? Or does time figure only vaguely in the living of our days? Are we always on time for meetings? Always early? Always late? For those who are always prompt, prayer at precise times might feel like a very natural way to begin. However, for those of us who operate on some internal clock known to ourselves and God alone, we might do better to commit to four daily prayers without specifying exact times.

Set times for prayer may help some people pray as they eliminate the constant deciding: *Do I pray first or do this job? Do I run an errand first, then pray before my meeting, or after?* Others thrive on such deliberations and may be more likely to pray with consistency without the constraint of particular set times.

The best way to determine which is the wiser course for you is to run the experiment. A day or two may not be adequate, and so, for perhaps a week's time you might attempt to pray at set hours, say, at eight in the morning, at noon, at four in the afternoon, and then at nine in the evening. As this becomes familiar, you may find yourself anticipating prayer, savoring the prospect of a sweet communion with your Savior breaking into the bustle and tedium of your day—for that is surely the complexion of our lives. But, it is not unreasonable to think that as we live into our new daily rhythm of devoted time with God, our *bustle* may give way to something more like calm and order; our *tedium* may become infused with interest and attention. If this sounds like too radical an expectation, we have only to look at the New Testament Epistles for specific descriptions of the kind of life we are actually offered in Christ Jesus.

It is a truism for writers that if you tell yourself you will write every day at 9 a.m., when you do sit down each morning at that time, you will often find you are ready to hit the deck running. If instead you write on whim at random times with neither planning nor anticipation, you may find that getting started is a tougher slog. It's how we all work: we experience the things that happen in our lives in fantasy beforehand, in reality as they occur, and in memory afterward. Anticipation sets the stage, and we respond based upon our past experience. That which we look forward to and that which we remember have a direct influence upon what we are doing in the present moment. When it is a given that each day we have scheduled four times to pray, whether these times are fixed or fluid, we come to our prayers primed and expectant.

There is nothing magic about set hours. Our schedules and our lives vary as greatly as our temperaments and our relationship with time. Commitments and conference calls, appointments and demands define the hours of some days. As you set out to begin a new daily practice, the most useful way forward is to try both set hours and fluid times and see which offers best compliance and times of truest receptivity for you.

Sweet Hour of Prayer

"So you always wanted to be an astrophysicist," the TV announcer says. "Seven years of schooling, seven years of training after that. No wonder you gave up. But now, good news! Thanks to a wonderful new program, you can be what you want to be. No, not with grueling years of study, slavery, and serious loss of sleep, BUT, in just five short minutes a day, you can achieve your . . ."

We click the remote, change the channel. But later in the evening, we listen with some interest to a best-selling author tell her story—to our own and the interviewer's amazement—of how she wrote her first book, two or three hours at a time, late (sometimes very late) each night, sitting at the kitchen table after her children were asleep. She finished it in three years. We don't change channels until the famous author is all done. She's accomplished *the possible.*

But we—the very same we—sit smiling and nodding the next time we hear somebody say, "God loves you. Spend time in prayer, even if it's just five minutes a day. That's all it takes. We can all do that."

I'm writing from the far side, fifty years down the beaten track, and from this vantage I'm convinced that this advice—the five-minute prayer program—is just as silly as the astrophysics ads.

Do we honestly believe these all-too-frequent advertisements that the God of heaven can be worshiped and comprehended, tapped for sweet communion, in just five fast minutes' time? Who wants to surrender all you are or ever hope to be to a God who will fit neatly in so small and miserly a space? What kind of saints are fabricated in five minutes? The same kind perhaps, with about the same quality, skill, and worth, as that instant and imaginary physicist who will never design a single spaceship.

Make no mistake, we are made saints at the moment of our salvation, in the twinkling of an eye, by the life-giving, soul-transforming atonement of Christ Jesus on the cross. But we work out our own salvation, and we grow in grace and in the knowledge of our Savior every single day that follows, for the whole of our lives.

So how long does it take to pray? It is a question worth asking.

Fast-forward to the end result: what sort of prayer life are we after? That's easy: living every moment of our fretful lives in blessed, precious union with our God, living in *him*—not in some religion or theology or discipline, but abiding in our Savior, *practicing the presence*, all day long, so that, finally, thought is prayer and the channel of two-way communication is open, unobstructed, and in good repair. We want to grow to see God everywhere in everything and praise him all the time. We long to arrive at that place

We long to arrive at that place of continuous connection, unbroken fellowship, where every breath breathes in his love, breathes out his majesty.

of continuous connection, unbroken fellowship, where every breath breathes in his love, breathes out his majesty.

It's hard to specify the time that this might take, though it seems safe to say it's probably longer than five minutes. The more time we spend with God in prayer, the more he will provide the answer to that question.

Someone's Dying, Lord

Spending time with God in prayer is not always effortless and natural. I find sometimes when I am praying, time weighs heavy. At those times when prayer does not come easy, I have been known to ask God for activity, for marching orders.

"Tell me what to do," I pray. "I am too restless here."

And God answers, in one voice or another, in a flash or after days and days. He answers with an impulse, a thought, or an odd idea—as often as not, one I have never had before.

"Dear Heavenly Father, tell me what to do," come my words one early morning hour as I sit in my chilly study with a scratchy blanket on my lap. "Oh, please, God, time weighs so heavily on me."

"Look at the clock," his soft voice says to me, not in a voice that's audible, but one speaking to my thoughts. "Someone is dying. At this moment." I sit up straighter, shiver slightly, and pull the blanket closer. "Someone is dying," his voice says. "Pray for her, for her immortal soul. For her salvation and safe passage. For peace, my peace, at the last."

I sit for several minutes praying for a stranger, for some-body God created and watched over for a lifetime, every blessed day. Then a new and seemingly random thought oc-curs to me: *Someone will die in precisely thirty-seven minutes.* I look up at the clock. *At 7:05 on the dot someone's life on earth will end. For good. Forever.*

"Sit here with me for those thirty-seven minutes," the voice comes again. "Pray that soul home."

I lift that life to God in prayer, and then it hits me: *What if that soul is me? What if I have been given notice of* my *death, a premonition of* my *end?*

Somebody dies every minute of the day. One minute, one day, will be my minute, my day. One hour—one God knows—will be the hour of my death.

I shudder with a sudden fear that I cannot explain, and then I really pray, the way I seldom do. I pray first for myself, and then, without any thought, I begin praying for everyone I know, every person on this earth whom I hold dear. The minutes pass, the circle widens. I am praying for people whom I hardly know; some are no more than names I've heard. And each and every one I pray for in the same way I would were that soul slated to die this cold November morning at 7:05 a.m.

And when I am done praying, I look up at the clock. 7:06. It's over. The time has come and passed. I am alive and well. I put my arms out wide and stretch. I give a mighty sigh. Time to get on with my day.

But oh, how fervently I prayed this morning, and with what sharp intensity. I prayed for me and mine in full awareness that today, or one day very much like this one, I will sit and wonder why I cannot pray and what I'll have for breakfast, and I will die. (I think that may be the first time in my life I've written down those last three words.)

The British playwright Ben Jonson said that even the prospect of our being hanged concentrates the mind magnificently. So might the knowledge of our mortality inform our prayers, enlarge our gratitude and praise for our salvation, and fortify our intercession for the world Christ died to save.

I think that how much time we spend in prayer depends on how successfully on any given day we whistle in the dark. So much of our attention and devotion is focused on keeping ourselves distracted, assuring ourselves that we are fine just as we are with no help from God or anybody else. To the extent that we can create diversion, especially through busyness, we can be comfortable not praying. But let even a thought remind us

How much time we spend in prayer depends on how successfully on any given day we whistle in the dark.

of what frail things we are, and prayer becomes a different proposition.

I remember visiting the town of Haworth near the Yorkshire Dales in England, the town made famous by the writing sisters Emily and Charlotte Brontë. Visiting their house and church and well-stocked churchyard, I couldn't help being struck by an awareness of the pervasive coupling of death and religion. Everywhere I turned that day there were reminders of the immediate presence of death and of God in the daily lives of the Brontës. The death of children was a more than common thing in that place and time, and even those surviving childhood often died very young. And, almost as a package deal, it seemed as though the history of this village was the story of so many brief lives, and the story of people for whom God was very close and real.

It struck me in such stark contrast with our own experience, where death is delayed at any cost, and, when no cost will be enough, where death is shrouded in denial and disguise. Even reading these words, I imagine the unconscious response might be a little spot of irritation: *What is this woman talking about? This is supposed to be a book about prayer, not dying.* As though the two were separable. If we are given a presentiment that this life will one day end, it can open up our hearts to hints of something more magnificent beyond the daily swirl; if we can catch a scent of glory, we might be helped to pray prayers more immediate and real.

Praying has everything to do with time. Time sets the limits, builds the boundaries of an hour, of a day, and of what will finally be a lifetime. Prayer would be a different thing if human life on earth went on forever; prayer will be a different thing in heaven, freed of limits, boundaries, endings, and death. Every prayer that's prayed is in the context of some level of awareness that time ends things—us, for instance. And time itself is on a collision course with eternity. *If* we pray and *how* we pray will be influenced not just by an awareness of our clocks and schedules, but by our knowing that both we and time will die.

I don't think this is macabre. The fact that we will die in order to live in love with God forever is a pretty compelling argument for beginning to know God right now. The fact that we will die, and that we know it, is one of the best aids to prayer there is. How often we pray, how many minutes we give it, will be directly related to how honestly we think about time's ending, how clearly we imagine the day that *forever* comes to be.

A Simple Little Total-Life Evaluation

Over the course of a lifetime, we hear hundreds, if not thousands, of wise and worthy sayings, but only a certain select few will seem to stick like glue. For me, one such phrase was spoken at a dinner I would not have attended knowingly. (It's a problem I have: not reading the fine print—and sometimes, not reading the large print.) I didn't know till I was seated at a table across from the evening's speaker that I had come, unwittingly, to a talk on fashion. I, who believe that God invented blue jeans so we wouldn't have to think about such things, was about to get the scoop on *what to wear*, as though perhaps a small committee had met privately and hammered out the guidelines. As my wardrobe will convincingly attest, I learned no fashion tips that night, but the speaker did say one thing that to this day is etched onto my brain.

She began by saying that we will all die with to-do lists. She noted that our lists seem only to grow, never to shrink. And so, her wisdom was this: *Accept the fact that your to-do list will never be completed, and so, while you are whittling away at it, make relationships the centerpiece of your life.* This wise woman—dressed, I must say, most becomingly—suggested that we might trade in the frank *impossibility* of ever finishing a to-do list for the entirely *possible* endeavor of forming relationships that matter. I may not have her phrasing precisely as she spoke, but I'm quite sure of the meaning.

> *Trade in the frank impossibility of ever finishing a to-do list for the entirely possible endeavor of forming relationships that matter.*

When it comes to our to-do lists, there is a behavior we persist in without rhyme or reason. With no evidence whatsoever that we can, or will, complete our list of tasks, nevertheless we get up every morning determined to give it *just one more try*. Every morning. Every day of our lives.

But what if, instead, we got out of bed and said, "Today while I am nibbling away at my to-do list, I'm going to keep my focus centered on being with God and other people in ways that are loving and important, growing in bonds that will last for time and all eternity"?

We think we will stop running when we're finished, but we're never finished, so we never stop. Yet, in the face of overwhelming evidence to the contrary, we actually believe at some point in time we will be all caught up; we will be no longer busy.

It might be tempting at this point to rush to resolutions to replace our list-bound days with lives of deep connection, love, and friendship. Hardly anyone would argue with that plan. And hardly any one of us would succeed in an attempt to make it happen. Every human behavior is predicated on some foundation. And so, if we are to change the things we do, we must first look at why we do them. The most practical, down-to-earth, nuts-and-bolts steps we take toward any change will be founded on some mighty big questions: *What is the meaning of life?* That sort of thing. We might not ever articulate our answers, but they determine much of what we do.

What is my purpose on the planet? What will matter as I lie dying? What does the world need that only I can give? And also other questions that lie closer to our hearts: *Does God really love me? Does anybody love me? Do I love anyone?*

Let's go back to our to-do lists for a minute. They offer such great clues about our answers to these questions. What does my list say about *me?* Hmm. I'm thinking if some archeologist came upon my to-dos a few hundred years from now, that nice little bit of distance might give great perspective.

Computer repairs, grocery shopping, exercise, finishing an article, balancing a checkbook, filing applications, buying shoes, calling the plumber. Where is God? Where are the people? It goes without saying that our relationship with God and our relationships with other people are all tied up together in many major ways. You might want to grab your own to-do list and see what it might have to say about the foundations of your life.

If we find ourselves at all attracted to this notion of *uncommon* prayer, we must first deal with the fundamental beliefs that underlie our actions. The unexamined life had its critics long before Thoreau took to his woodland hideaway; even before Aristotle declared the unexamined life not worth living. If we have not figured out the *why*, it will be so much harder to create the *what*.

I Want To, But My Life Won't Let Me

I would love to say that my own prayer practice went swimmingly forever, once it was begun. In point of fact, across a number of weeks and months, my four daily prayers became three, then two, then one, until some mornings I would rush out of the house with quick promises to myself to pray later—promises that could get submerged by a couple of unexpected phone calls or a well-earned case of exhaustion.

Does this mean that I sat down and evaluated the particulars of my sojourn on the planet and decided it was in my best interest to skip praying? Hardly. I was not reasoned—I did not reason myself—out of my four-times-daily prayer practice. I just started letting prayer take a backseat to everything else. It isn't that we don't want God; it's that we want something else more. I think the thing that I want more than prayer is not a late-night movie, or being there for my kids, or coffee with a friend, or even finishing work on a new novel. I believe the nature of desire is far more subtle, and the forces at play much trickier, than that.

There is a foundation underlying the decisions that I make, and that bedrock is my wanting to believe that my life as I find myself doing it, living it out day to day across the years, is a thing that is not determined by me. I want to believe that my work and family and the whole of my life are not under my control. I'd love to be a better person, I really would. I'd love to be patient and rested and orderly and yes, even disciplined—so disciplined that prayer could easily find a place of priority inside my days. *But*, my life won't let me. It is as though I believe some irresistible force compels me to be other than I would desire. This belief alone could make me take a job I hate, make me work to pay for things I may not want or need. It makes me respond to the phone every time it rings—I'm helpless. It makes me check my e-mail forty times a day and answer every one. It makes me cater to my family, to my friends, and to virtual strangers who call me up and ask if I can bake things for a sale. I believe that life is what's happening to me while I am making other—far, far better—plans. I want to say that I didn't make my lifestyle, that I did

45

not design the life I'm living. I am a little fuzzy on just who it was who did, but the thing is set in motion and I must obey. "Oops, excuse me, I have to take this call."

After all, what is the alternative? That I awaken tomorrow morning looking at sixteen waking hours that God has given me and choose myself what I will do with them? That I go to bed tomorrow night—or on the last day of my life on earth—and I say, "This is what I chose to do with that one precious day"?

"I have to . . ." seems to be the start of every sentence that I say about my time.

Just for the fun of it, I make a list of the things on my schedule today that I do not feel are up to me to decide upon: Two hours installing *Dragon Naturally Speaking* so I can dictate writing onto the computer. One hour tidying my house (I *do* choose *not* to vacuum) for a meeting here tonight. Taking a walk with a friend. Meeting the cable guy to fix the TV. Going to the gym. Cooking. Taking six phone calls and reading fifty e-mails. Reading the *Times* online. Checking Facebook.

I do not believe these make anybody's list of most sinful behaviors, but I do believe my life is lived in such a way that it is very hard for me to acknowledge that all these things are optional, that I have actually chosen each and every one. Maybe it's just my innate desire not to be lonely, but I'll go out on a limb here and suggest that I might not be the only person in the known world who thinks this way, who believes my life is not up to me.

It is entirely possible that you might awaken tomorrow morning and spontaneously begin to pray at four set times each day, and continue that discipline until the day you die. However, just in case this particular miracle does *not* occur, what follows is a very practical approach to discovering some things about your life and then instituting a new prayer practice based on solid understanding.

It is entirely possible that you might awaken tomorrow morning and spontaneously begin to pray at four set times each day, and continue that discipline until the day you die. However, just in case this particular miracle does not occur, what follows is a very practical approach . . .

If we take it as a given that we must reorganize our days, free up time to pray—time already occupied with other things—this can lead us to a nicely directed way forward. No day is sitting empty, waiting to be filled. We must first take a hard look at the activity already in place. It will tell us much about how we view our purpose on the planet, and in the end will help us make decisions about fitting time to purpose.

What I am about to suggest here is a little exercise, very mechanical and practical, but one that I think holds out the offer of some very useful information. So, to begin:

1. You'll need paper and a pen—perhaps two pens—and a large dose of honesty. The first step is to write down

everything you did yesterday. No need to find a quiet time and place for this part of the exercise; just start the list and keep adding to it as you remember details. And it must be yesterday. To catalog today's activities might subtly influence your choices in some ways. It is imperative for this little exercise that we start with the most reliable information we can get.

2. Once you have yesterday's list as detailed as you can make it, begin a second list of everything you've done in the past week. Whereas the first list is highly detailed, this one can be done with broader brush strokes. (An interesting side note to consider is the number of hours in the past week that we discover we're hard-pressed to account for. What does it say about our being present in each moment, that we can recall so few of them? We cannot remember what we were not aware of in the first place. Distracted at the time, we do not register experience. It is not there to be recalled.)

3. The next task, once the lists are finished, will be to make two columns on a blank sheet of paper. The first column will be labeled *MY CHOICE* and will include those things you *chose* to do. The second column is labeled *NOT MY CHOICE* and will list those activities you *had* to do, those things over which you had no control. Take the lists you made for yesterday and for the past week and assign each item on the lists to one column or the other.

Now, I suggest you age the list for two or three days. Set it aside in order to allow yourself to gain a little distance from your designations. Time is a lovely resource, often working wonders when we allow ourselves to move away from any project, to stop thinking about it, so that we might return with a fresh eye, with some less-familiar, more-objective perspective.

4. After a few days, sit down and read the assigned lists again and see if any of the items on the *NOT MY CHOICE* list might actually fit better under the heading *MY CHOICE*, which enumerates those things that you chose to do. Be as honest as you can with this step. It may not be as easy or straightforward as it seems.

5. Now, you address the things remaining on the *NOT MY CHOICE* list. Beside each item, write the name of the *decider* for that activity. Since it wasn't your choice, whose choice was it? For instance, an activity might be put down to health or family, to contracted obligation, to employer, to emergency, or to pressing need. Assign a name to the decision maker for each one. Since you yourself did not choose, who or what was the chooser? Identifying the deciders in our lives, who they are, what rules they make, and how they cause us to obey, could change a life.

6. Finally, devote a bit of time—yes, that time that is in such short supply—to an evaluation of the lists you've made. The way you approach this might take many forms. You may decide to sit in prayerful silence and consider a number of questions:

   ❧ What do your lists reflect about your goals? Your priorities? Yourself?

♣ How do your lists answer the overarching questions, the ones that really matter?

♣ What do they tell you about how you understand
the purpose of your life?

♣ What information do these lists provide when what
you do all day, all week, is reduced to this accounting?

♣ Who are the *deciders* in your life? What gives them
their authority?

♣ Which ones might you choose one day to disobey
or even to eliminate?

♣ Might you want to move toward acknowledging
that a lot of choices are in fact your own?

We don't determine what our lives will be in one deci-
sive moment. Our lives are crafted by the tiny, hourly decisions we make, small, seemingly inconsequential choices
that shape and mold us. Which items on our lists will have
reverberations for eternity? Cleaning a bathroom in faithful
service to others might well resound forever, while a moment of public triumph might last for just as long as that: a
moment.

This meditation on our choices calls for a fierce honesty
as well as openness and precision. Take nothing as a given,
but hold each activity of your day, your week, up to the light.
See it for what it is. Ask its worth. Determine its value and
honor as well as its service to God, to the world, and to your
own soul.

❧ Does a particular activity honor God and draw my
heart to him?

❧ Does it provide for the good of other people?

❧ Does it enrich my spirit?

❧ Does this activity form me as I want to be formed
with the mind of Christ?

❧ If I do it every day for all the days of my life, will it
move my heart in a heavenly direction?

And finally, a question suited to our purpose here: Is this
activity more worth the doing than is prayer?

Owning Our Lives

As we focus on the choices that we make, it is important
to acknowledge that there *are* ironclad, irrefutable demands
in every life. This is a fact of life. But there are fewer lives than
we might imagine where this is the case for every hour of every day. It has been said that even in concentration camps the
prisoners had choices, if only to choose the spirit in which
they walked to their executions. Yet, I can't remember the
last time I heard anybody say, "This is what I'm choosing to
do today."

Based upon nothing more than a good supply of years of
watching what I do, I am convinced that living a life of true
discipleship begins with one foundation: acknowledging that
much of how I run my life is indeed my own decision. "The
devil made me do it" wasn't much of a defense in the garden

of Eden, and it still sounds like the echo of the first-grader caught with his hand in the cookie jar.

One of the most substantial changes we can make is claiming the ownership of our lives. God has given us each a precious gift: time. Time made up of little minutes, days made out of hours, swiftly passing years we shake our heads at, wondering where they've gone. When we stand before our Maker to give account—and yes, word is that's still the plan—we will not be allowed to say, "My life stole my time away. My schedule, my commitments, my daily life did it, not me. My existence came in the middle of the night and stole my years from me." We can do with ourselves what we will. God created us in just that way. What we cannot do is say we have no say in the matter. We pray. We don't pray. But we get to choose. We will not stand up on the Resurrection morning and give as our defense: "It wasn't my call."

We have a choice all right. The problem is we do not want it, because if we ever reach a point where we acknowledge that the lives we live are the ones we craft ourselves, then we are face-to-face with what is overwhelming and impossible. Then we know we are incapable. We are weak and wanting. It is a hard thing to own up, to say, "Here's my life; this is what I decided to do with it; here's what I have made it be." No life will measure up to any standards, be they our own, or others', or the Lord's.

We would be thrown then upon the daily, hourly, minute-to-minute mercy of God, and we would know it. It is far more inviting to say, "You know, I'd really like to pray more, if things were different, but my life's demands won't let me have a say."

We need to own our schedules if we ever are to change them.

We need a change of thinking as much as we need a change of heart.

Chapter Four
HOLY DISCIPLINE

A NYONE WHO HAS SPENT MORE THAN fifteen minutes in adulthood knows that discipline is a sticky wicket. For openers, once we decide on a course of action—be it praying, or losing a pound, or walking more than a hundred feet a day—all the natural force of opposition kicks in. Just the act of stating an intention seems to summon a resistance we never knew was there.

I'm inclined to deal with this by trickery. I'm easily fooled, thus making this the obvious approach for me, but I hope that you might also find it a useful strategy. The steps I use whenever I'm intent on getting myself to follow through with something new involves a little spot of self-deception.

Say I want to walk three miles a day—it's no more than the truth. It is at this point that my *self-talk* and the truth part company. If I tell myself it's time for my walk, the phone rings—that is, the phone of the person I call to talk with about something that suddenly seems urgent. Faced with the prospect of exercise, my otherwise faulty memory starts working like a champ. Instantly, I am reminded of twelve things I simply have to do, and right away.

So. My trick. First, I tell myself—convincingly—that I do not have to exercise, now or ever. That lowers the bar considerably. The soothing reassurance flies in the face of my expectation that I exercise for an hour every day for the rest of my life. Then I tell myself that while I do not have to walk an hour, I do have to put on my socks and sneakers. That's it. That's all I have to do. Once I am properly shod, I say that while I do not have to walk an hour, I do have to step out onto the front porch. Nothing more. Just that. And so it goes. Once outside, I have only to walk to the end of the driveway. Then, I'm done. Once there, I have only to take a few steps and I'm finished. You get the picture. At some point, I'm on my way. After one of these baby steps, I am walking, and the lunacy it took to get me going won't be needed until I get back home and am faced with some other daunting project I am positive will be too overwhelming to ever attempt.

If this strikes you as beyond pathetic, then you may be blessed with a self-discipline that makes all things possible. However, if you find the idiocy of this at all appealing, you may—as I have—find that beginning a practice of praying four times each day will be easier if you make use of this mini-steps approach. When, for whatever reason, I am not inclined to pray, I tell myself I do not have to but I *do* have to just go sit down in my prayer place, or open the hymnal and sing one line of just one hymn, or find the matches and light just one candle. Tiny steps. They can serve you well. They serve me beautifully.

The First Seven Seconds

Much about our having a new life of prayer involves habits, the ones we have and wish to lose, and the ones we long to gain. I happened to catch a segment of a program on PBS. It was a talk by a scientist who had studied the nature of self-discipline, among other fascinating functions of our brains. He told the story of wanting to change his own habit of coming home from work each day and clicking on the television as he entered the living room. Based upon his clinical findings, he believed the first seven seconds are the critical interval that determines whether, or how easily, we carry out any habitual action. With this in mind, he took his remote control outside and put it in the glove compartment of his car. The next day when he came home from work, he sat down, and reaching for the remote control, found it wasn't there. He realized he would have to stand up, cross the room, open the door, and go outside again to get it. Just that short, intervening time and effort needed to perpetuate his habit was enough to create an interval of time for him to stop and consider: Did he, in fact, want to watch TV at that moment or not? That day he broke a habit that had held sway for years.

Similarly, to help institute a new behavior, he gave the following example. This scientist had always wanted to play the saxophone but found he just never had the discipline to do it. So, using the seven-second boost for starting or stopping any behavior, he set up his music stand with the sheet music on it and put his saxophone out on the dining room table, thereby eliminating the first few seconds of preparation needed to practice his music. What he found was that just having that small barrier removed, the sheet music and saxophone already in place, made it possible for him to start playing; and so he has done, every day, for the last twenty years.

It shouldn't be so simple. We want it to be harder. (Then we can say, "I can't. It's too hard.") But if we want to pray in a new way, to lose old patterns of being and put new ones in their place, here we have two useful models. The first is to take steps to interfere with habits we are longing to displace. If every morning the first thing we do is check the news, we may actually need to do a bit of disabling of the electronics that bring us the first distraction of the day. If the daily habit is to set up the production line for lunch boxes for seven people every morning, might a new habit be to do this chore at night? Silly as it sounds, if the kitchen is the room that waylays us on our way to pray, a piece of bright blue painter's tape across the light switch might be all it takes to get us through the kitchen to a prayer spot in another room. I am suggesting we are more easily led than we might like to think.

Promptings

If we want to institute new habits in the place of old ones, the setting of the scene for morning prayer can remove the seven seconds' worth of setup that constitutes a barrier we are often hard-pressed to surmount. Before we go to bed, if we open a Bible, put a lap robe on a chair, against the early-morning chill, and set the coffeemaker at the ready (yes, for some this might be a prayer aid like no other), such tiny steps can actually make us more likely to sit down first thing in the morning and pray.

I am a big fan of the timer. One would think that high noon might readily call itself to my attention, but I can look up from work and see it is suddenly 1:45 in the afternoon. A timer sounding a call to prayer is something that I often need. I love the idea of the ancient bells that through the centuries have called people to prayer. I find the simplest of prompts helpful. I might put my coat in some unlikely spot as a tickler to remind me to head off for my midday prayers outside.

And so too for late-afternoon and evening prayers. I try to remove the triggers and the wherewithal for habits that interfere with prayer, and I might put physical props in place as well. The smallest things can call us: an open book, a wooden cross, an altar with a tiny flower in a vase, or a candle burning. What works for one may be useless for another; but for us all, the strategic use of preventers and prompts might very

The smallest things can call us to prayer: an open book, a wooden cross, an altar with a tiny flower in a vase, or a candle burning.

likely outwit us in enabling ways. And for those of us for whom a calendar is what keeps us steady in the water, we should by all means write down prayer appointments. "Notes to self" stuck on a bathroom mirror can make the difference between prayer and no prayer.

The reason these suggestions are not more specific is that each one of us works differently. We must observe our habits, get to see them clearly, if we are to ever put new ones in their place. It is hard to overstate how individual this will be, this journey we are embarking on. There are those for whom prayers and hours will be the prescribed liturgy and times of the church throughout long ages. For others, prayers will assume every sort of variety and timing. And across the years, it is likely practices will change and grow. There are seasons in our lives; and needs, and ways, and circumstances will have their say.

So, a prayer life will be tailor-made, individual to us, and flexible and changing as need says it must. That is the practice we are called to design. The creative aspects of this are so fine and fitting. Our Creator calls us to invent in every dimension of our lives, and prayer is no exception.

Tweaks and Tryouts

Trial and error helps immeasurably as we move forward. If every night at ten o'clock your prayers are interrupted by complaints about your snoring, you may need to tweak a bit. Pray standing. Walk outside. We live in bodies. Don't ignore them; make them work for you. I found it very helpful to make a program of prayer at the beginning, a framework into which I might move seamlessly. I prayed with Scripture in the morning, went out of doors at midday to revel in God's creation, and then sang rousing praise songs as catapults to worship in late afternoon. Psalms, Gregorian chant, and candles led to prayer at the close of the day. This simple form gave way to every sort of interesting variation, but it was a solid starting place for me.

Some practices might even feel like gimmickry, but I believe that prayer is developmental. We start where we are, in the simplest ways. We move into different stages as we learn to pray, but always at the start prayer will be halting, strange and new.

Disciplines at first are hard. We feel self-conscious, awkward and unpracticed. Then something happens. What we do habitually becomes a brand-new habit, automatic and reliable over time. We develop habits that are so much a part of us we are no longer aware of them. The power of habit is a force we want to harness for our good, for if we are not busy praying, we will be busy doing something else.

To view a day, any day, in any circumstance, as a thing to be structured gives a useful rhythm. Unless we stop intentionally and plan, we will be carried along by the flow of the day. The hours pass, lockstep, unstoppable, whether we plan them out or watch them pass as though we are observers. Observers of our days. Observers of our lives.

Whatever form we may choose, it is far easier to follow through when prayer is planned. Would we interrupt a meeting to go pray? We would do it for a dental appointment. Would we cut short a coffee date for prayer? We do it for a class. We tend to honor our commitments. What if we committed to certain times to pray?

And, of course, we must bear in mind that habits are no more than a roadway. We must not make a god of our habits; we must not worship structure or daily practice or any spiritual discipline. In the end our goal will be to move beyond habits, growing in relationship and love. To make a habit of being in the presence of our God, to make a habit of knowing and loving him—that is the end we seek.

Chapter Five
THE PRACTICES OF PRAYER

P RAYER IS NATURAL, INSTINCTUAL, WITHOUT RULES or boundaries, while at the same time it can also feel complicated and demanding, sometimes downright difficult. I can remember when I was in college sitting in a tiny study room having my *quiet time*, feeling much like a kid who had been sent to her room. I sat there for the regulation twenty minutes, all but twiddling my thumbs. Being told to pray without a clue of how to go about it is something like being given a new baby in the hospital with not so much as a two-page owner's manual. Although prayer, and parenting, can be automatic and intuitive, there is also much that can be taught to brand-new parents and to novice pray-ers.

Across a lifetime prayers can take every form there is, from silent listening to ebullient praise, from desperate, piercing pleas to dumbstruck adoration. As I began my new daily plan of praying four times each day, I found it very helpful to try different practices, a number of which I want to share in hopes that one, or some, might lead you to ways of being with God and opening your heart in his holy presence.

Some practices will sound perhaps a bit mechanical, some silly, others even awkward, or odd—perhaps outside your comfort zone. But comfort zones are highly overrated. *Comfort zone*: the name we give to the ever-shrinking little space where fear, timidity, and selfishness corral our possibilities, confine our aspirations, and severely limit whatever use we might be to the world around us. There is, of course, a comfort we will find in prayer that is true consolation, but it is expansive and freeing, so unlike the restricting comforts we manufacture for ourselves by limiting what we do and how we do it.

I suggest you might like to try each of the ideas I offer here, even if only once. These ways of praying will be done without any human observation or critique, and neither should you rush into the void to evaluate and judge yourself. Any new practice will feel strange at first. Don't judge; just do. Experience the variety. Give thanks for the richness and the depth it can bring.

The Ceremonial

I believe that our attention, mood, and concentration in any sphere are affected by ceremony. It calls us from routine, from our rote reactions, our knee-jerk ways of moving through a day. The smallest nod in the direction of the ceremonial alters our awareness of what we are about. I find it helps me to designate a chair to use only for prayer.

I discovered one day, quite by chance, that putting a prayer shawl around my shoulders helped me focus and relax as I stood by a tiny altar—nothing more than a small table in the corner of my dining room on which I placed a wooden cross. The chair, the shawl, and the altar each signal that this is to be time marked out as extraordinary. Kneeling, bowing, standing, and dancing to the Lord all enlarge our worship, as does our creating any sense of ceremony and occasion.

Our physical surroundings can play a part in preparing us for prayer. Years ago, I visited a precious friend, Tim Pearson, when he was a student at the University of Massachusetts. I opened the door to his apartment to find him standing on a kitchen chair taping Bible verses in a boldly printed frieze all around the walls of every room. I went home that day and looked around my house, wondering at the prompts and reminders I had put in place. Cut glass; willow-pattern dishes; curious hedgehogs made of clay, and glass, and wood—quite the contrast with Tim's showcase of the Word of God.

Those whose days are spent caring for others may want to institute specific times and practices of prayer together with the ones they care for, there to mark out with special observance times spent consciously in the presence of the Lord. Praying with children—and those men and women with young children may only rarely be able to pray in solitude—often invites a special kind of "ceremonial." Children love habit and the specialness of ceremony. Parents may choose to gather the children in a special corner at noon, or four o'clock each afternoon, to pray. This can become an honored ritual, a special time that children may well come to anticipate and relish. Prayer shawls, soft lighting, music, and kneeling will all help to signal that what is being done has meaning. Parents should indeed try to find pockets of quiet for prayer that is truly alone, but gathering your children with you in prayer is not a second-best option, to only be included when you cannot find solitude. Our children know the things that parents value. I've read that adult children most closely espouse their parents' faith at the level at which the parent actually believed and lived, not at the level at which the parent taught. I have a friend who prays and reads the Bible with his teenage son before his son leaves for high school every morning. "Does your son like it?" I asked. "I don't know," he said. "I don't know if he likes it or not, but when he is an old man he will know for certain what mattered most to his dad."

Tune My Heart to Sing God's Praise

Music is integral to prayer. In the Old Testament, the prophet Elijah is asked to pray in order to receive a message from the Lord about the outcome of an impending battle. At first Elijah says no. Finally, he agrees. "OK," he says, "bring out the harps"—that is, "Begin the music that will bring me to the place where I will hear God's message." Music transports us to a state in which we are receptive to feeling. We let down our defenses; we release our tight control. Music *acts upon us* for our good.

I often stand alone in a chilly room (I live in New England and keep the thermostat at 58 degrees) and sing out loud. In a thin voice that sounds so often tinny to my ear—some days scratchy-sounding, some days clear, with notes more true—I sing hymns. All four verses, all eight verses. I figure inasmuch as we will sing in heaven, we might as well get started memorizing all the verses while we're here. I believe the songs God loves are the ones sung from our hearts, when nobody else is there. Imagine how you'd feel if a loved one sang a song to you.

I sing the old, warhorse hymns, weighted down with wisdom, Scripture, and enough theology to carry me through a day. And as I stand and sing, I pray, "Dear God, hear my little song. I am singing it to you." It helps me to hear myself, my feebleness, my weakness and dependence on the One I worship. I know my offering for the puny thing it is, and I know a God who accepts it as sanctified worship.

We still sing psalms every Sunday in my church. And I find that in my private prayers, singing psalms helps me to slow down and focus on the ancient verses, the psalmist's words that cover every human circumstance. Lamentations make up two-thirds of all the psalms, but there is also praise, instruction, wondering, and understanding, bedrock certainty and wild confusion in the psalms we can sing every day when we pray.

I also find that playing praise songs on Pandora on my computer, or on a CD, sometimes allows me to close my eyes and rest, and move into awareness of the Lord with me in the room. At other times, the music makes me sing along and raise my heart in feeling and devotion. Music, as well as visual art and poetry, can be a great remedy for those of us who live too much inside our heads. The synchronicity of soul, and art, and song is yet one more demonstration of the fascinating way God has created us to work. We are designed to respond to music; we are made for song. The reason any work of art can move us is that God made us creatures so affected in this way.

Music can rouse us or quiet us, depending on what we choose to play. Sometimes I put on songs of worship for ten or fifteen minutes as I work around the house, before I stop to pray. And then it is music that moves me to worship, that gets me ready. Washing the dishes, I am Elijah in the kitchen, saying, "OK, bring on the harps."

Scripture Reading

Whether we tape it on the walls or write it on our hearts, Scripture surely has a critical role to play. I try to begin each morning's prayers with Scripture. My reading style is not one I recommend, but I share it here to illustrate that God works with us individually, as quirky as we are. When I open the Bible, I often read at random, and usually pretty quickly some curious element will send me off in exploration. I use a study Bible and frequently find myself moving back and forth between the Testaments as I pursue the references I'm given. I find this randomly structured study most often has profound effects, leading me to one conclusion that I often speak aloud: "Oh, Lord, so that's what you are like."

I'd be hard-pressed to recommend my practice. Surely choosing to read more systematically will be of greater use to most. But no matter if our reading is random or orderly, one rule applies: less is more. Focus, in your prayer time, on short sections of Scripture; it is hard to meditate on several chapters at a time.

Considering the Ravens

Often after I have spent time in my own peculiar inter-action with the Word of God, I come away with a verse or phrase that I try to stay with during the day. Memorizing any words of Scripture, no matter how few, always helps us to pray and to remain prayerful as we move through a day.

"Consider the ravens" (Luke 12:24) stuck with me all day yesterday. I found it puzzling and engaging from the start. It made me think of a flock of blackbirds, or perhaps they are a *murder* of crows or an *unkindness* of ravens—I love those classy classifying names—who on occasion congregate in my backyard, pecking energetically at something only they can see. However, yesterday they were obviously busy elsewhere; not a single raven came around to be considered. Later in the day, driving home on autopilot, my attention was arrested by the sight of a dead possum lying, furry and intact, beside the country road. *Consider the ravens. Consider the possum.* In that moment I believed God cared about not just the ravens but also that possum's life and death. Tears filled my eyes when I realized that God loved this creature he had made. *Consider the ravens.* Could it be God loves me as much as he loves them?

When we read the Bible in prayer, we are meant to take it personally. We can read each book, each verse, and with certain benefit ask the question, *Why did God write this to me?*

Here, of course, the Bible, like any other thing, is not immune to misuse. I remember as a young girl hearing the story of a woman seeking divine input; she closed her eyes, opened the Bible, and put her finger on the line that would tell her how to proceed. As the familiar story goes, the verse she blindly chose was, "Judas went out and hanged himself." Trying again for clarification, the second verse she touched was, "Go thou and do likewise." So much for Scripture out of context.

Reading Others' Words

Through words written down across the ages, we have access to our history in the human family, to our story as the sons and daughters of God. I've heard it said that we should always be reading something written at least fifty years earlier so that we are not misled into thinking that our own limited cultural moment comprises the ultimate understanding of things. Personally, I would expand that fifty years by five or six times more. Both my feelings and my apprehending have been wonderfully blessed by spending time with such spectacular thinkers as John Owen and Jonathan Edwards.

Reading writers from another time can do a great job of getting our attention. These writers do not speak the way we do; their perspectives and references are born in daily lives that we have to stop and wonder at. This helps, I think, to cause us to consider the question: What are the common elements we share? What is the nature of *timeless* Truth? William Law, writing a good three hundred years ago, single-handedly changed the time that I get out of bed each morning. Though his culture feels like another world to me, the hours that make up a day are just the same in my world as in his, and his writing convinced me that prayers offered early in the morning spring from one imperative down through the centuries.

Reading devotional writing can surely *lead* to prayer, but make no mistake: such reading is not itself praying. For myself, I can easily sit down and become absorbed in a great book *about* God and substitute that for being *with* God. Such reading is integral, blessed, and for me I feel essential, but it is a struggle for me not to allow it to become a substitute for prayer. This is my own struggle. We will each one have our own.

Praying in Our Bodies

I cross myself.

Not all the time; not with any regularity or pattern. But now and then the impulse takes me, often unawares, and my hand touches forehead, heart, then shoulder, shoulder, left to right.

Making *the sign of the cross.*

And when I do, it *touches* me, *reaches* and *involves* me. Every single time.

I spent the first eighteen years of my life in the Christian and Missionary Alliance Church, and then headed off to a Wesleyan Methodist college. For the past twenty-five years I have been Anglican. (My son, who was reared as an Anglican, is now a pastor in the Church of God, the denomination of my grandparents in the 1920s. What goes around does indeed come around.) All of which is to say that making the sign of the cross is not something I grew up with. I was first introduced to this practice in a lovely gray stone church, watching every service as this particular phenomenon was displayed. After certain words, before this or that phrase or prayer, everybody present fashioned invisible signs of the cross. Some made swift, efficient crosses; some separate, miniature ones on forehead, lips, and heart. For years I sat and watched, and then one afternoon, while driving home, stopped at a traffic light, I made one too.

And I made a discovery. It is a simple act, but *doing* it is different in some way from *not doing* it. There was something about that slight movement of my hand that seemed significant—not casual, not ordinary. I did it again. I spoke the words aloud "Father, Son, and Holy Spirit," with an image of covering myself with the blessing of God the Father, God the Son, and God the Spirit—a prayer, immediate and real; a blessing, pervasive and substantial; a covering I could feel.

The driver in the next car gave me a thumbs up. The light changed. I drove away.

But I learned something that day, or I started to. And it is this: What we do with our bodies as we pray is of importance. Praying on our knees is different from praying standing up, or lying down, or sitting. Each posture comes with attitude. Each one *feels* different from the others. But it is more than feeling.

We live inside of bodies; we take them everywhere we go. God himself created us that way. So why must we pretend that it is a matter of indifference what we do with them in worship, that they are somehow excluded when we pray?

We are not our bodies, but we live in them. They influence us; we influence them. An intricate relationship exists between the sometimes-disparate parts that make us up.

If we raise our hands to heaven when we sing, hold our hands out, open, when we pray, it is different from if we do not. Our physical acts play a part in prayer and worship.

In the movie *Windtalkers*, two World War II, Navajo, code geniuses observe carefully choreographed ceremonies of prayer and worship, at sunrise and sunset, every day, no matter where they are or how the battle rages around them. In solemn concentration, they move and pray with purpose and imperturbable serenity—their movements part of prayer, their prayers involving all the parts of who and what they are.

Observing the gravity and impact of this portrayal of prayer made me wonder, what part do our bodies play when we are with our God? I stumbled across my own answer quite by chance. As therapy for chronic migraines, I was told to meditate, and I was given exercises to do every day—a stretch for a sloth like me, but pain's a great enforcer. One day I realized I could do these exercises while I did my meditation. (A diehard multitasker, it's a wonder I didn't try to knit then too.) And so it began. It was never precisely clear what moment meditation ended and my prayers began, and so, gradually the exercises too began to cross that fuzzy line. My prayers of praise and petition came with certain movements.

Shoulder circles backward found companion language: "May I cast all my cares on him." Ankle circles moved with: "So that I may walk with grace the path set before me." Stretching right to left became: "May I turn from sin and cast my gaze on you." Arm circles said: "I praise you for your creation." High stretches overhead said: "Praise to your majestic glory." Each movement became a part of prayer, each act involving all of me in worship.

The Old Testament often speaks of dancing to God. I haven't gotten as far as that in my devotions, but I can say that praying with my mind, and heart, and body is a blessed thing to do, not artificial or self-conscious, but right and purposeful and true. Movement helps to concentrate my thoughts; standing before my God, head bowed or looking skyward, hands out or arms raised, seems to physically remind me what I am about. My kneeling prayers are blessings of a very different kind.

This is no robotic, mechanical adjunct to our conversations with our Savior, but rather prayer with every attribute we possess. It is presenting "bodies as a living sacrifice that is holy and pleasing to God" (Romans 12:1). It's never isolating these "temple[s] of the Holy Spirit" (1 Corinthians 6:19) from our prayer.

From that first afternoon at the stoplight, I have crossed myself thousands of times, each time making tangible to me the grace of God. An Eastern Orthodox priest told me that he touches his thumb to his index and middle finger when he makes the sign of the cross, the three digits touching, one more tangible expression of prayer to the Three-in-One Deity. This too has become reflexive when I cross myself, which I do now even when visiting other churches. Sometimes I am the only one doing it. In many congregations, making the sign of the cross is not a native practice. Perhaps it should be, not by rote, nor in response to a formal signal, but in the ordinary moment when the heart cries, "Bless me, Father, Son, and Holy Spirit."

Glory be to the Father, and to the Son, and to the Holy Spirit.

Glory be.

Making the sign of the cross has been a common practice since the second century; it was a seal of sure protection in both the books of Revelation and Ezekiel. It is a symbol of deliverance, and a cry for help; an emblem of God's mercy, and an act of worship. It is prayer without words.

Fasting

Prayer and fasting. The phrase might not be the first thing that comes to mind in this regard, but it is a coupling we are taught in Scripture. Let me say emphatically—I never hesitate to state the obvious—that what I say here on this subject comes from my own squirrelly brain and is in no way meant to represent the thoughts of God or anybody else. Because of my particularly pesky blood-sugar requirements, I need the influx of new calories about every two hours. Let me go three hours without eating and I'm not a happy camper, and neither is anyone who happens to be nearby. At such times, strangers routinely offer me random foodstuffs along with reassurance. I do not fast. I absolutely believe that if I did, God would be entirely capable of keeping my blood-sugar levels where they should be; but I do not fast.

I believe there are many physical conditions that make fasting from food something other than an ironclad mandate. But, the Bible is full of references to fasting. We are told to fast and pray. It seems to me that food is only one of the things that I can fast from, and it is not the hardest thing I might give up, not by a long shot. There are far more difficult things for me to abstain from when I pray.

I've learned a lot about fasting from observing the season of Lent—my favorite season of the church year. (I think a person does well to have a favorite season in that holy calendar; it means there's always something to look forward to. I wake up in the morning on December 26, Boxing Day—not a church holiday as far as I'm aware—sniff the morning air, and sigh, "It's almost Lent." I adore Lent, that season leading up to celebration of the Resurrection morning.)

Lent and fasting go hand in hand, but I'm not talking about giving up chocolate. My yearly practice is to give up TV, because it is a thing I notice when it's gone. In addition, one year I gave up not trusting God for Lent. One year I gave up being depressed. One year I gave up saying no to party invitations. I offer these as illustrations of things I fast from for a season, but there are also things I fast from when I daily pray: e-mails, phone calls, books (for me the hardest thing of all). As I say, these are no more than my thoughts, but I am sure that for every one of us, there are things far harder to give up than food. Removing those things from our focus and involvement for a time can surely help us pray.

Praying Others' Prayers

Collections of prayers written by others can help us mightily in the shaping of meaning and intention in our prayers. Other people's prayers can be the cure for the meandering mind, the antidote to daydreaming. One particularly helpful series is called The Divine Hours, by Phyllis Tickle. There are four of these books of prayers, one for each season of the year. Each book contains daily prayers and readings for morning, midday, late afternoon, and evening. I found this a particularly helpful resource as I began my daily practice.

I have many other anthologies of prayer on my book-shelves: *A Diary of Private Prayer* by John Baillie, *The Book of a Thousand Prayers* by Angela Ashwin, *Handbook to Prayer* by Kenneth Boa, and a very worn and tattered ancient *Book of Common Prayer*— no bigger than my hand, its micro-scopic print including even the lyrics of the beautiful old hymns. Rather recently, I found a most unusual prayer book when, quite by happenstance (that is, if we believe in happenstance), I came upon a brilliant collection of Puritan prayers called *The Valley of Vision*. This book has helped me concentrate in prayer like no other I remember. I mention this book not by way of recommendation—I could imagine it sending someone else running screaming from the room, Puritans being an acquired taste—but rather as an illustra-tion of amazing and *providential* provision that God sends so individually suited to a particular person. There are books of prayers that I can read and attempt to pray, only to discover that I have turned five or six pages without registering a single word. But somehow the prayers Arthur Bennett has collected and edited in *The Valley of Vision* arrest my atten-tion with each brief phrase or line.

Allow me to give an example from this particular col-lection of just how a book might influence our prayers. This book is divided up by themes, with repentance comprising one entire section that has been so wonderful for me. In the Gospels, John the Baptist heralds the coming Christ with one central word: *repent*. It is where the Gospel begins.

Repentance. It's where we start. "God be merciful to me a sinner" (Luke 18:13 KJV) is the precise prayer that Jesus commends. It is the place of our entering in. I could never have gotten to the state of amazement, that gateway to adoring worship, without a free home demonstration of my sinfulness. I read this ancient prayer book's prayers of repentance gaining awareness and conviction of my sin.

By using this prayer book day after day, I have been helped to learn that the magnitude of mercy will never be clear to us, the nature of amazing grace will never change our hearts, until we have reached the self-understanding of the hymn writer of "Amazing Grace." That man, John Newton, wrote an autobiography in four words: "a wretch like me." Modern conjurers attempt to reinvent reality, and so they substitute the vaguely intentioned word *soul* for *wretch* in the song's second phrase, but we are nowhere near the heart of prayer until we understand ourselves as wretches—and wretched at that—those beings so lost that nothing short of the death of God could save us. If we are "not so bad really," then grace is not amazing. Nice enough, but hardly earth-shattering. Every word we say in prayer betrays our theology, and collections like this one nail with precision the understanding of who and what we are.

There is no set program for communion with our God. There is relationship, and that is one unique to every soul. We are not offered the generic model of the interplay between God and everyone. We have one God, one faith, one baptism, and one Savior's gospel over all, but we have a one-to-one experience of our lives in Christ. We know ourselves to have unique human relationships with all the different people in our lives. No two are identical. And so it is with each of us and God. He knows and loves and relates with me as me, and with you as you. Prayer is the joyful discovery of the nature of that bond, a bond that will brand us, mark us as Christ's own, forever. Nevertheless, it is wonderful to sit and read and pray prayers written by another person that feel as though they were composed for us alone to pray. There is a rich sense of community in praying written prayers, a bond with those whose praises and petitions voice what our hearts long to say.

> *There is a rich sense of community in praying written prayers, a bond with those whose praises and petitions voice what our hearts long to say.*

Although two-minute prayers are not a substitute for our dedicated, focused prayer times, I have discovered that just picking up a prayer book a number of times throughout the day does wonders in keeping my thoughts and moods and actions on the course I long for. This is different from the "Please bless . . ." prayers that spring unbidden through the day as I remember any special need. Rather, as I read these prayers, and also sometimes the words of hymns or Scripture, my thoughts are redirected. The language instantly removes me from the task at hand, even if only for a minute, and allows my heart to worship. I return to whatever it is I'm doing in the light of that instant blessing. If there is one lesson we must learn, it is that worship changes everything. To give thanks, to praise God and adore him, in focused concentration even for a minute, does something to us—something done no other way. This is no substitute for prayers of dedicated time, but it is a sweet addition to have reminders of God sprinkled through a day.

The good news is that the world is full of prayer books. Just ask Google. Typing in those two words will reveal enough to keep us steady in the water for the ages. I thank God for the rich profusion in this particular department, knowing that we each respond so differently, and that what serves us well at one time may not at another. As is true with everything we read, we find that what opens up our hearts and minds one year may find us in the next scratching our heads and wondering what all the fuss has been about. We have shifts and changes, seasons of the soul, each with different temperature and weather patterns. I am persuaded that God uses so many different means to keep our thoughts and spirits where they must be when we pray.

Pray God may guide us as we explore these and so many other possibilities, as we say the words, "Lord, teach us how to pray."

Praying Scripture

As we live into our commitment to a new life of prayer, I offer one promise: there will be surprises, serendipitous fine-tuning of our practice that will come as providential mercy, as outcroppings of grace. It goes without saying that not one of these surprises will be unprecedented in the history of the world. We are blazing old trails here, ones strewn with mercy, revelation, and wonder; ancient trails traversed by better pilgrims than we might ever be. I take that as the good news. I love knowing that we are indeed surrounded by "a great cloud of witnesses," men and women of prayer, and yes—let me say the frightening word—*piety*. (The word is now all but completely dedicated to the hypocrite, the exclusive purview of the modern Pharisee, whose day job seems to be the policing of everybody else. But I'm thinking it may well be time for a return to some more common dealings with the word.) The fact that we discover ancient disciplines, those practices that have served the truly pious—there, I've said it again—through the ages, does, I hope, give us encouragement. It can be taken as a sign that we are on the right track, offering certain evidence of the spiritual connection within the body of Christ. Here is a reminder that we are one with all the saints through all the ages, just as we will be when the world is seamless; when experience is no longer cut up into centuries and hours; when that strange divider—time—no longer limits our interplay with what is real.

Although we will invent no untried ways of praying, as everything we do has been done before, nevertheless, it will often, and blessedly,

Old new. New old.
Glory be to God for
oxymorons.

feel brand-new to us. "[God's mercies] are new every morn-ing" (Lamentations 3:23 KJV). The more time we spend with God, the more we will experience this as true—true in ways that are flat-out delightful; true in ways that feel so tailor-made to suit our needs we can't believe it. Old new. New old. Glory be to God for oxymorons. Prayer stripped of novelty would be a boring thing, I think; prayer bereft of history, just fanciful and jury-rigged.

Old New Mercy

To illustrate, I'd like to share a miracle, for so it truly feels to me. Not long ago, on one remarkably bad night, I found myself not only unable to sleep but also unable to settle down. My thoughts were racing, though they certainly weren't going anywhere. Rather, they were wearing a deep groove in one endless circle, and all my usual efforts at distraction couldn't interrupt the spin. In desperation—that is a word that earns its name—I tried repeating individual Bible verses to my-self, to God, and to the late-night kitchen. I thought of verses that spoke to my particular midnight moment. And, without any planning, I began speaking them as prayers. "Let your strength be made perfect in my weakness. Let me take every thought into captivity in obedience to Christ." The verses lined up in an orderly fashion as I repeated them in sequence over and again. More verses found their way into this sponta-neous litany. Each time I added a new verse, I repeated them all in the order in which they had first come to me. I spoke them over and again, and I found myself becoming calm and centered. "Clothed and in my right mind" is a phrase I've always liked—and certainly aspired to on that troubled night. As I prayed the Scripture, a soft peace spread around me.

As I said, there's nothing new here. God's word is more powerful than anything else we might experience at midnight, or 3 a.m., or any other time. Oh, but it was new to me that dreadful night—and some nights are truly dreadful, let us not pretend.

Since that night, no matter how often I have repeated this particular collection of verses, it is no rote prayer that I pray. Because each verse is freestanding, I have to stop and think before each one—a slippery memory can be a lovely aid to concentrated thought. The verses anchor me in prayer as I am forced to stop and think which verse comes next, and so through the weeks and days to follow I find myself praying this same prayer with honest concentration. *My* prayer. For so it seems to me to be the prayer *I* need to pray. It comes to me on daily prayer walks through my neighborhood. By the time that I have prayed it just three times, I find that I have walked a mile in true communion with the Lord. One segment of my prayer is the Gloria:

> *Glory be to the Father and to the Son and to the*
>   *Holy Spirit,*
> *as it was in the beginning, is now,*
> *and will be forever, world without end. Amen.*

And with the words I make the sign of the cross. I bless myself. I bless my neighborhood. The Holy Trinity is evoked and blessed now every time I walk around the block.

I am certain any number of brain scientists are lining up all eager to explain how physical phenomena can easily account for my experience. I find these arguments that are intent upon removing God from the equation do in fact accomplish just the opposite. We—our brains, our bodies—respond as we do because the magnificent Creator designed us in order that we would. We have been created to respond to certain stimuli in ways that calm and bless. We are "fearfully and wonderfully made" (Psalm 139:14 KJV), as the most casual examination of any newborn's eyelashes and fingernails will reliably attest.

There is no better argument I know for memorizing Scripture than this: it may form our prayers. I grew up in a church where children were rewarded for memorizing Bible verses by the score. I'm thankful to those faithful saints now with the Lord for the consistency and discipline they brought to the endeavor. Encouraging—and yes, rewarding—children for learning Bible verses by heart is a gift we can offer to all the children in our lives. Children memorize so easily, and what is committed to memory in childhood often stays with us through life. *Learning Scripture by heart* is surely, always, prayer.

> *There is no better argument I know for memorizing Scripture than this: it may form our prayers.*

84

On that dreadful night when Scripture verses formed themselves into the prayer that held such meaning for me, such deep worth and blessing, I added verses as they *came to mind*. I would have been hard-pressed to read and search for verses on the night in question. But I didn't have to; the stockpile was in place because some western Pennsylvania Sunday school teacher in what seems like another lifetime bothered to make sure I learned God's Word by heart. We teach our kids so many different things; please, God, may Scripture verses always be among them.

Lectio Divina

I have only learned in recent years of the ancient practice called *Lectio Divina*. *Lectio Divina* is a Latin term that means "divine reading" and describes a way of reading the Scriptures in which we intentionally open ourselves to God. There are various ways of practicing *Lectio Divina*, but most follow four basic steps of reading, meditation, praying, and contemplating. The first stage, *lectio*, or reading, involves choosing a short passage of Scripture to be read slowly and reflectively. The second stage is *meditatio*, or reflection, a time of sitting quietly, considering the text we have chosen, and meditating on its meaning and richness. The third stage is *oratio*, or responding, when we put thinking aside and speak directly to God in response to what the Word is teaching our hearts. The final stage of *Lectio Divina* is *contemplatio*, or rest, a time when we let go of everything and simply rest in the Word of God.

I am part of a small group that meets monthly for *Lectio Divina* for two hours on a Sunday afternoon. We sit silently for the first half hour while the leader of our group reads a short passage of Scripture, usually no more than five or six verses. He reads the passage three times, allowing quiet of ten minutes' time between each reading. We then sit silently, sometimes with journals if we wish to write, and we reflect on the reading. We allow the words and images to penetrate our hearts, to touch us, to speak to us. We invite God's Holy Spirit to help us respond to the reading, and, finally, we rest in God's holy presence as the day draws to a close. At the end of each meeting, we share very briefly anything that God has been saying to us. The sharing is without comment or any discussion. The atmosphere is reverent.

In *Lectio Divina* we listen at the deepest level of our being to God, who speaks with a still small voice. As we listen, we are acted upon by the Spirit of God. This will have a profound effect on the way we actually live, which is the test of the authenticity of our prayer. The practice of *Lectio Divina* can be done in many different ways, alone or with other people, but always with a clear-eyed, openhearted concentration on the Word.

As we discipline our hearts and minds in prayer, Scripture will always be a necessary standard and corrective. We all are prone from time to time to get a little too creative. When we encounter those aspects of Christian living so very counter to our natures, we naturally attempt to put some lesser standard in their place. In addition, living life surrounded by a culture that is alien to the gospel, we are constantly invited to conform our lives in Christ to the sensibility and customs of our environment. Our very prayers can be influenced and shaped by the world around us. It is for this reason that Scripture must always be a part of prayer. As we read any Bible text, we can turn its words into the foundation for our praise and petition. God has given us words that we can read, and contemplate, and pray. Without his Word, we can surely lose our way, even as we kneel to pray.

The Place of Prayer

Just as we will choose the many different ways we pray— as well as the times—we will also choose the places. Sometimes life helps with the decision. On certain days a train, a work cubicle, or a hospital room will be the only options. That said, I think we fool ourselves a bit when we attempt to pray while we are actively engaged in another activity. Surely we can be consciously in the presence of the Lord when we're behind the wheel of a car, but it is fair to neither us nor the driver in the oncoming lane to devote our full attention to prayer when the path of true discipleship demands we focus on the road.

At the times we do get to choose where we pray, some say it's best to always pray in the same spot, perhaps a room, a corner, or a chair you use only for prayer. Certainly it helps to have a place that your mind associates with being conscious and receptive in the presence of the Lord, but it is also true that there are times when novelty helps us to pray. Being in a different place, one that's new or strange, calls us out of the daily, common patterns and gets our full attention. I find this is particularly true in my case. Even at home, standing in the middle of a room where I have never stood to pray can help me focus and become more aware that here I stand ready to engage in something that is outside the daily run of things.

Being outdoors in any spot with the conscious intention of praying always helps me to focus. For a long time my practice in the late afternoon was to walk to the college campus near my home and stand beneath a large oak tree overlooking the small pond. Even the walk to get there seemed to set the stage. *Where are you off to? I'm off to meet the Lord.* I have also discovered that the more places I go to pray, the more this increases my awareness of God's being present everywhere. As I move through my day I have the specific memory of experiencing God's presence in so many different places.

> *I have also discovered that the more places I go to pray, the more this increases my awareness of God's being present everywhere.*

Driving by a deserted cornfield late one autumn afternoon, I pulled over, parked the car by the side of the road, and walked some distance between the dry brown stalks until I stood with nothing but the soft blue sky for cover, nothing but the clouds for company, with no other human element in sight. And there I stood and belted out the song:

> All hail the power of Jesus' name!
> Let angels prostrate fall;
> Bring forth the royal diadem,
> And crown him Lord of all,

my heart in honest worship.

It has been said that to the Christian, all nature is sacramental. Often something as simple as looking at the bare limbs of a tree against a winter sky can bring me to a state of awe. I can't say how many times I have been brought to earnest awareness of God by looking at a mighty, towering tree and realizing that I know the One who made it. My friend Jenny shakes her head in wonder as she says, "I don't know how anyone can go to the zoo and not believe in God. Just look at the giraffe." All of nature, every creature, lives to God's glory and can call us to remembrance of him.

Looking for a new spot on rainy days might call for adaptation. I have gone out and crawled into the backseat of my car to be alone with God, when my thoughts were in serious need of some corralling. I never sit there otherwise, and so I'm more attentive there. The smallest, least consequential thing can influence us powerfully for either good or ill.

As with choosing prayer practices and prayer times, deciding on places is something that calls for some exploration and experimentation. Trying out different practices, times, and places gives us good information. And always, we must remember life is a patchwork of vicissitudes and circumstance, needs and preferences, in continual flux. Every discipline of prayer is a work in progress, changing as we find our way directed and enabled by God's Holy Spirit.

Chapter Six
WRITING TO GOD

G OD HAS GIVEN ME A WONDERFUL OCCUPATION. I am a fiction writer, and part of my work time these days is devoted to mentoring other writers, those who are brand-new and taking tentative first steps, as well as those who are seasoned pros. These men and women, at whatever age or stage, have one thing in common: they have all been taught the adage "Write what you know," and sadly they have taken the advice. And to them, I offer the antidote "Write what you don't know." That is, I encourage writers to begin with their questions, not their answers, to approach their work with bold uncertainty, with openness and frank perplexity. Be it a novel or a story, a poem or an essay, the way in is always a wandering pathway. Writing is a meandering endeavor. When we approach our creative work with conclusions, our art can feel lifeless and formulaic.

And so it is with our prayers, which are in their truest sense the enacting of our relationship with God, just as our conversations are the essence of our relationships with the people in our lives. Approach a teenager with pronouncements and watch her vanish before your very eyes; but come to her with interested inquiry, with genuine wondering, and all things might be possible. It is the nature of conversing. To make declarations is a very one-sided affair.

There are two ways to come to God: *open* or *closed*. If we approach God with our conclusions and decisions, with our fixed opinions and ironclad beliefs, at some level what is there to talk about? Prayer is a venue for questioning; it is a place for probing, for exploration and examination of interest and desire. The reason we sometimes complain about a prayer life that is dull and routine, the reason in truth we fail to pray, may have something to do with our beliefs about prayer. If prayer is sitting in a quiet corner asking God to bless and heal and give, it is a one-way street—one that is not long or very interesting.

The disciples lived with Jesus day in and day out across hundreds of stunning days, and still they said, "Teach us to pray." Can we do any less than put some time and effort into being taught? The schooling finds us on our knees. It is our God who will teach us. But we need to show up, and we need to kneel or sit or stand in honesty. We need to come as we are, not as we pretend to be. Most of us spend a fairly large part of our lives pretending, in ways we are not even conscious of.

Honesty and openness are where we must begin. And here I will suggest that language plays a part, that what we say to God and how we say it, how thoughtfully we think and speak with him, is a matter of importance.

We have only to think about the marriage where a busy woman says to her spouse, "Good morning, thanks for being my husband and being so nice. Thanks for going to work and for the sweet kids we've got. Would you please take the car in today, call the plumber, fix that garden hose, make dinner (pretty please), and help John with his application and his algebra? Thanks! I love you. Bye." And that's it for Monday, with Tuesday's conversation pretty much the same.

Bland is not interesting. Routine is not enthralling. Words spoken automatically do not engage the speaker or the listener. Don't get me wrong: I do not believe that there is one prayer we utter that is not heard by God. But I do believe that there are prayers we utter that are not heard by *us*, that we who speak them without heart engagement some-times barely register the prayers we pray. I learned that praying in silent thoughts, praying in spoken words, and praying in written lan-guage produce three very different kinds of prayers. The very first time I tried writing down my prayer to God, I was surprised by the honesty, the questioning, and the sincere engagement that appeared as I sat writing in my

> *I learned that pray-ing in silent thoughts, praying in spoken words, and praying in written language produce three very different kinds of prayers.*

little spiral notebook. Speaking and writing call forth very different aspects of thought and expression. Try writing to God just one time and you will see the difference.

Here are a few sample prayers from my heart and pen. They are often confused, and rarely eloquent; they ask questions freely, but are not tied up with easy answers. Many prayers in the Book of Psalms do not conclude with tidy resolution. The prayers here represent my attempt to come to God in honesty, to stand before God in Christ by the power of the Holy Spirit, for once not pretending. These are one woman's words to God, her Father—words expressing gratitude, alarm, and wonderment; bafflement, interest, and devotion.

Those who teach the ways of prayer will speak of writing prayer journals as well. Such journals might be written in a myriad of ways, but all will serve as a record, a diary, of prayer. These compilations of our praises and petitions can be of great usefulness. The most surprising thing for me about a prayer journal is what happens when I return to it, months, or even years, later. I often find these prayers perfectly suited for the moment when I revisit them. I can pick up an old prayer journal and pray with fervor the lines I wrote in another time and place. So a prayer journal will surely be part of every practice; however, what I am suggesting here is something a bit different. As you read and pray the prayers here, and then as you begin to craft your own, you will discover that this discipline of writing words to God involves precision, concentration, and even editing—all practices that sharpen and define for you what your heart wants and needs to pray. To imagine that praying is always off-the-cuff spontaneous is like imagining a lifetime of conversation where you speak first and then think. Make no mistake, there are frequent times when we pour our hearts out to God, in silence, in speaking, in crying, and in journaling. But deep, concentrating thoughtfulness also has a place in prayer.

We write all our prayers in the very presence of God, being guided and directed and instructed by him even as we put each word on paper. There will be no rules as you set out to craft your own prayers, no restrictions or limitations. All you need is an open heart and a pen and paper—sometimes even a napkin or an old envelope will do. I find that these prayers often come to me at unexpected times. It makes good sense to take them down before they are forgotten. I keep my crafted prayers and pray them over and again, sometimes returning to them years later to find them appropriate to the moment, fresh and seeming new.

I invite you to pray some of these prayers with me, although not all will be your prayers, I know. But I hope that these might be a model for the prayers that you will come to write yourself, prayers that are as particular to you as these prayers are to me.

My Prayers

The first prayer I share here was written in a dentist chair, evidence we can write fervent prayers no matter where we

are. I waited till the drilling was all done, and then sat in the
waiting room and scribbled down this dental-chair prayer:

> *Dear Lord, It's me here in the dentist chair.*
> *They've put the words* root *and* canal *in the same*
> *sentence . . . again. I'm deciding whether I will be*
> *alarmed. Yes, I think I will be.*
>
> *And then I open up my scrunched-up eyes*
> *and there you are beside the chair. You do not look*
> *alarmed at all.*
>
> *So, what if I decide not to be afraid till you are;*
> *not to let anxiety take over like some sneaky bully,*
> *not until I see you tremble; not to let fear rocket me,*
> *until I first see fear in your eyes.*
>
> *Dear Jesus, hold my gaze, and if I start to turn*
> *my head, please reach out and touch my chin. Don't*
> *let me look away.*
>
> *I pray in the name of the Father, and of the Son,*
> *and of the Holy Spirit. Amen.*

This next prayer is a conversation that I needed to engage in. Not all prayers I write are sleek and streamlined. In
fact, it may be fair to say that few are. Many of the prayers
I write are awkward and inept, but they are my attempts to
bring my thoughts and feelings to God in the very moment,
to lay out my confusion and uncertainty, to begin to wonder
in God's presence about the things that feel important.

Dear Jesus, I am hiding.

You call out, "Where are you?" and I step out decked in fig leaves and a mask I made myself. Fig leaves, in December, in New England. Masks that I pretend will cause you to confuse me with somebody else.

But even if I take the mask away and let you see my tear-streaked face, still, I will sew more leaves together, try to hide my nakedness. I spend all my time trying to get unnaked, trying not to look like what I am, imagining you will be fooled by me.

I only fool myself. And only sometimes. Only a tiny bit.

What if I ever stood before you as I am. Am I afraid you'd look away? There are things about me I do not want to know. Are you different from me? Would you say you loved me even so?

I can't take anything for granted. I really want to know.

I do not pray: "Please let me find you." I pray: "Would you please find me?"

I pray in the name of the Father, and of the Son, and of the Holy Spirit. Amen.

Some of the prayers I write are brief, but they are from my heart. I try sometimes to put down in words what feels like the very essence of the feeling or idea. I find these small prayers are often the ones that I pray over and again.

*Dear Lord, I want nothing more this moment
than to sit here in the stillness and to feel your light
hand upon my head. I am not good at being loved.
It seems I have more practice being on the sidelines,
watching loving from afar. How to be loved is something I will have to learn. I think I'd like to start today.*

*I pray in the name of the Father, and of the Son,
and of the Holy Spirit. Amen.*

There will be paradox, even contradiction, in our prayers. Things are not always simple, and they are not always as they seem. I find that when I write my way in, not knowing at the start where I will end, that I am often met with honesty and revelation. I believe when I sit down to write my prayers God speaks to me; he teaches my heart lessons that I need to learn.

*Dear Lord Jesus, I spend so much time every
day trying to be good, to do the right thing, to be
holy, even. But today I see that it is all about me. I
want to feel good about myself. I want to be satisfied
with me.*

I try to be good, I think, so you will let me be.

*But, over time, it gets tiring. It wears me out.
I never make the grade. How very much I'd like to
think I do not have to do this all by myself. Please
help me throw my hands up in defeat, defeat that
finally can be victory.*

I pray in the name of the Father, and of the Son, and of the Holy Spirit. Amen.

As you begin to write your own prayers, you must know only this: there are no rules. Spelling doesn't count. And neither do any other limiting requirements. To write prayers, you merely begin to put on paper what is in your heart. No form. No editing. Just taking down ideas and questions, praises and petitions. Later you might want to shape these into prayers that you might save and use again. I am no songwriter but I can easily imagine a person might well end up writing songs this way.

Am I a Poet? No

I sometimes find that when I sit in God's presence thinking on a topic and writing down ideas, what comes will be a poem, or something that I give that name. I have a very particular fascination with the hours on the morning Jesus rose up from the dead. I often try to imagine Jesus on that early morning before anybody knew that he was risen, and my thoughts might take a number of forms as I scribble them down.

Easter, Hours before Dawn

I can't see the clock. Is he up yet?
Who else shushed the angels? God
put the risen dead to bed last night

all tuckered out from two days back alive
while *he*
stormed the caverns
of demanded dooms,
made tombs
ridiculous.
But how can even he
rein in
the laughter
capable of parting seas
before the mountains were brought forth
or ever they had formed the earth and the world
that morning, so very like/so very unlike this
—the world has aged, and man.
But for today
they hang the morning star
in reach of children. He has already
pulled the covers from the corners of the sky,
made coffee, stoked the dawn, called home,
sat down to wait.
Tapping his foot.

Love isn't patient.

Risen, he might still rend the night.

Love isn't kind.

I find this theme comes back to me over and again.

Impromptu

Mary Magdalene comes to the tomb
on the first Easter morning,
Please sir, she says
—all polite now, dressed nice, hair combed,
demons exorcized—
*Please sir, they have taken my Lord, and I don't know
where to find him.*

Mary, Jesus says.
Just that. Her name.
But this comes later, after sorrow, after fright,
after the angel who's been waiting
since the afternoon that Lucifer reared up and flash
descended into hell, since before that even.

Jesus is not here.
The angel speaks, feels the words as he eternity-
forever thought they would be on his lips.
Jesus is not here.

The angel clears his throat.
You might want to check the morning skies.

Off script.
Again.

God shakes his head.
The angel giggles.

I believe we do well to stay with the images that come to us. I think there are good reasons certain times or places, characters or stories have a special resonance for us. I find I just keep returning, over and again across the years, to this one particular morning so filled with richness and mystery for me.

Easter Morning

We each one have our own
particular idea of
what hour,
say,
what minute,
the Resurrected
roused and stretched,
scratched and blinked,
hard, twice,
and arose.
From the dead.
We some have it
daybreak
when he soldiers forth,
a squirrel, a
Middle Eastern squirrel,
the tiny witless witness
of the day the world changed.
God loved one squirrel that much.

WRITING TO GOD

We some have him shake off the shroud
like silky cobwebs in the middle of the night,
feel deeply dew in darkness
as he first fills, refills, lungs;
feet, loving wet grass,
toes happy.
The whole world fast asleep.

(The book does say: resurrection of the body.
Resurrecting any other bloodless thing
I find of no interest whatsoever.)
So:
we will have body, blessed, boldly please.
Not only toes, but turban hair, cramp, wrinkle, myrrh perfume:
a drench.

Others have him rising later—six fifteen—
approaching dawn,
the witness, stumbling home,
a drunk
who does not know he's there,
who does not know he's there.
That is who God comes to,
dripping glory
on damp sand.

As I have said, I am a word person. Words are what I go
to first, last, and in the middle. It is hard for me to pass an

hour without reading or writing something down. However, when it comes to art or music, I am sadly lacking. We must each find the ways that best express ourselves in prayer. For one person, the act of painting may be prayer; for another, writing music may be what it is to pray. Not all the time, not every day, but sometimes, when there is no other prayer for us to pray, we make art. It's what we're made to do. I wish I had a nickel—or a hundred-dollar bill (I'm hardly fussy)—for every person who has told me that he can't write, he has never written: that's the evidence that person thinks will carry the day. But every one of us has trafficked in words, in language, since babbling babyhood. When we sit down to compose, we've got a running start; we've been practicing since toddler days. It's not like picking up a violin for the first time. It's using something we already have, but in a different way—that something being words.

Give it a shot. Sit down and write a prayer. Then get down on your knees and thank the Lord who allows us to create. It is a sweet thing altogether.

For twenty years I have led weekly writing groups. One thing I have noticed over these years is that no two people living write in the same voice. Indeed we might not need to look elsewhere for evidence of a splendid particularity in God's creation: everyone's voice is unique and surprising. I make a point of saying this here because I find so many who are afraid of writing. (The odd English teacher may have much to answer for.) I say to anyone who reads these words: give it a shot. Sit down and write a prayer. Then get down on your knees and thank the Lord who allows us to create. It is a sweet thing altogether.

Chapter Seven
HEARING GOD'S VOICE

A CENTRAL, BLESSED PART OF PRAYER IS LISTENING. And so it seems important to consider what we mean when we speak of *listening* to God, of *hearing* God *speak*. Here, as perhaps nowhere else, we need to be alert to pitfalls and true peril in our prayers. We have all heard people report direct communications from the Lord God, these being sometimes alarmingly specific and perhaps too often bearing a remarkable resemblance to the speaker's own leanings and persuasions. It's obvious why those in the convincing business might mark their words as being straight from heaven. It packs a mighty punch when we attribute an idea to the Almighty.

An editor friend advises freelance writers, "Please don't write and say the Holy Spirit says that we should publish your piece. The Holy Spirit may have sent us a different message." But this sort of representation is fairly harmless compared with pronouncements that can lead the believing far more dangerously astray. There is such potential harm, indeed, when one person—especially one who has more power—attempts to influence others by adding the heft of divine endorsement. In relationship with other people, I believe that we do very well to own our own ideas and not blame God for what it is we think. It is absolutely true that there will be communications direct from God, but, oh, it takes a cautiously discerning spirit to determine when that is the case.

There are more subtle aspects in private prayer for the individual who might confuse her musings for God's promptings. We must determine how we will distinguish our ideas from his. How do we know if it is God who's speaking to our hearts?

The first, most obvious, of answers is that any time God speaks, God's words by definition will accord precisely with the Scriptures. God will never contradict his own Holy word.

The second rule of thumb that I find helpful is to always err on the side of owning every thought as mine initially. I might feel promptings, nudges, or intimations that I believe are direct communiqués from God to me, but I try to always temper my perception with the words "I think." In any given instance, God may or may not be directly communicating with me. I can feel it keenly or perceive it as the faintest twinge. Either way, I say that *I think* God is telling me to do or think or be this way or another. The Apostle Paul in the Epistles makes very fine distinctions in this regard, saying *I believe* I have the mind of God on this, and then on other occasions declaring outright: *This is my own thinking here.*

I believe we receive confirmation that it is God who speaks to us in extremely quiet, unobtrusive ways. I remember being at a Bible study one night, and as I left the church I felt a strong and definite prompting to drive home via a route I never take. I drove out of my way, keenly on the lookout for God's reason for the detour. I arrived back home not having noticed anything out of the ordinary. As I walked into the house, I felt again the prompting, only stronger, to go immediately upstairs. I walked through every room on the second floor, but nothing was remarkable or different in any way. Then I had the sharpest feeling of direction to walk into the bedroom, actively and sharply in keen expectation that God was directing me. I was totally focused and attentive, on the lookout for God and what he was up to on that summer evening. But the room was just as I had left it. There was nothing to report. With a stronger and more defined prompting now compelling me, I knelt down beside the bed to pray, and heard God speak to me in the silence of my thoughts. He said, "You know the expectation, the looking forward, the openness and excitement of the last half hour as you trained your gaze to look around you in order to see me and what I might be up to?" And I replied, with hesitation, a quizzical "Yes?" God said, "That's how I want you to live your life—with the alive and tuned-in anticipation of my working in the tiny details of your day. I want you to see me, present and active. Everywhere you go, I'm there. Be on the lookout all the time."

Now of course I paraphrase, and for certain no audible words were spoken by me or by God or by anyone, but I believe that God was indeed speaking to my heart that night. This happened maybe fifteen years ago, and sitting here today, so far away from that house, that bedroom, in fact, that life, I can still bring back the feeling. I can still remember what it was like that summer evening, walking like a child on tiptoe, ready to surprise God at his work.

The point here is that it was an individual experience that touched me and changed me. It doesn't matter if anyone else believes that God was talking to my heart that night. Jesus heals the man who was blind, and when questioned, the man replies, "Here's what I do know: I was blind and now I see" (John 9:25). One test, I believe, of our sensing God's speaking to us, is to ask if the communication is quiet, rather confidential, and clearly so individual and instructional that it feels peculiarly intended to teach us what we need to know.

The Two-Way Street

I also believe there is a reciprocity in prayer. That is, if I had ignored the promptings as I left the Bible study at the church that night, I might never have received the message God had for me. One afternoon, I was cleaning out a closet, collecting things I didn't wear in order to pass them on so that they might be of use to someone. I liked the feeling of lightening ship, getting rid of things I knew that I would never wear. Then I came upon a sweater I had ordered online back in May and had forgotten about with the arrival of hot summer weather. I was so tickled. I'm not a clotheshorse, or even much of a shopper, but I was delighted with this soft white sweater with its interesting buttons and nice deep pockets.

Immediately came the strongest urging, "Donate that; put it in the pile for the survival center."

I would have chosen to give any garment rather than that one. I liked it so much. Over the next two or three days I carried on a little interior discussion of the matter. I am forever trying to talk God into seeing things my way. I reasoned, *Who really needs that? Who would love it as much as I? Could I donate it and send away for another just like it? Would I give it and then get one as a gift soon for being so generous? Why give the only one I care for?* But no matter what arguments I mustered, the nagging message was always the same: *Give it away.* No doubt. No amendment.

"What shall it profit a man, if he shall gain the whole world, and lose his own soul?" (Mark 8:36 KJV).

Not much.

Finally, unable to ignore or to refuse any longer, I folded up the sweater and put it in the donations pile, and in that very instant the prompting changed.

"Take it back. Wear it. Enjoy it. And when you do, every blessed time, let it be a reminder of God, of my faithfulness and loving-kindness to you. Let it remind you that like the sweater, he holds you and wraps you in his protective love and mercy."

I wore that sweater for years, and every time I put it on I felt God's caring. I could never have known the comfort or the blessing till I put the sweater on the pile.

How Can We Tell God Is Speaking?

When God does speak to us there will be hints of confirmation: other people, circumstances, results from our obedience, fruits of that industry, and, sometimes more quietly, nudges that will not leave us—particularly nudges that are counter to our own inclinations; ideas that will not let us be; offers that we can't refuse.

I also believe that the more we devote not just our time but also our very selves to prayer, the more we recognize his voice, and the more softly he can speak. It is a given that the Holy Spirit of the Lord may not speak to us indefinitely. "[His] spirit shall not always strive with man," we are told (Genesis 6:3 KJV). "Grieve not the holy Spirit" (Ephesians 4:30 KJV). We must not ever think that we can disregard God's messages and messengers at our fickle whims and our persnickety convenience and have the option of responding when it suits us. At those times when we feel God is dealing with us, ready and available to teach, and reach, and train, we cannot turn away, imagining that we will be inclined another time. God is the instigator here as everywhere. He is the actor; the agent; the initiator. Let us never think it starts with us. If we

God is the instigator here as everywhere. He is the actor; the agent; the initiator.

desire to approach him, if we sit here now in this moment reading a little book about prayer and find ourselves wanting to pray, we can be sure God's hand is in the enterprise. It is a scary business to ignore his overtures, to pretend they will be always there. We all know from experience that there are times when we are open to God's Spirit with tender hearts and open and receptive minds, just as we know that there are times when we are closed for business, times when God is a vague abstraction we barely know is there.

As a rule, when I feel a prompting that is for the good, I tend to go with it, assuming that even if I am mistaken about God's directing, the people whom my actions bless won't care much where the idea came from. For example, one day it seemed that I should go to the supermarket with the decided and entirely conscious intention of doing someone good. Thoreau would have had a fit—he, who said he'd run like the dickens if anyone ever came knocking on his door purposing *to do him good.*

I walked into the store that morning determined to change the overall complexion of some unsuspecting stranger's day. I found my victim waiting in aisle 11—a scruffy-looking guy in shabby clothes, standing fixed, examining the batteries and light bulbs. I circled back four times till I was sure he hadn't come to shop, had not the wherewithal to buy. I routinely decide such things about strangers: their overall plentitude of cash, friends, family, or dinner plans, based on not much more than posture, facial features, and wardrobe choices. I blame it on the fact that I write fiction for a living. I am very accustomed to making things up.

"Excuse me." I called this unsuspecting soul from his intent perusal of the AAA long-life batteries. "I wanted to give you this." And I held out a slender roll of bills.

"No. No. I don't need anything." With these few, flustered words my victim was halfway down the aisle, with me in hot, now fully crazed, pursuit.

"I'm sorry. I just wanted to give you . . ." I said.

"Stay away from me." He vanished down the aisle of bottled beverages.

You stupid, stupid, stupid jerk! I thought. *Who died and left you in charge of being Lady Bountiful? You stupid fool! You idiot!*

By now I was at the border between produce and baked goods, hiding by the sweet potatoes, resting my full weight against the counter holding up the yams and me.

Idiot!

And then it was as though I heard God say to me, "Did you do this to please me?" And I said, "Yes, I actually did." And God said, "I am pleased."

Still, I looked around for somebody in management who would very soon be asking me if I might shop elsewhere from now on, and then I saw him. My poor prey, not far away, intent on selecting the perfect banana. He was giving them his undivided attention, but I knew he knew I was there. Slowly he moved in my direction, looking elsewhere, till he reached the piled potatoes.

"Actually, I really could use that money," he said, "if you don't mind."

I handed him the damp bills, still clutched in my hand.

"Thank you. Very much." He moved quickly then toward the exit, turned his collar up, pocketed the banana, and left the store.

As with most of the experiences I'm sharing here, this story does not fall under the heading of suggestions. But I tell it here because I think sometimes our willingness to follow subtle promptings is a part of prayer. We are earthly creatures, transacting all the living of our days in broken—ever-breaking—bodies, in humble circumstance, in simple ordinary arenas of behavior, surrounded by people and things of the most common sort. And I believe that God wants us to respond to him only in the simple ways he's placed at our disposal.

I think that our actions—our simplest, sometimes most childlike actions—can be acts of prayer, part and parcel of our communication with our Lord Jesus. I believe so deeply that God speaks to us in circumstance and through other people as we take tiny actions in the world in response to the promptings we might feel.

> *Our actions—our simplest, sometimes most childlike actions—can be acts of prayer.*

Don't get me wrong. Prayer is not all dollar bills and random acts of kindness. But prayer is provision of the good we sometimes apprehend only in symbols. Jesus instant-aged some mighty fine wine to make a wedding party (John 2:3-8), and so too can we in smitten devotion to the Lord give to others that which blesses them. We offer everything we've got. We do it in devotion. That's the plan. And there is nothing random in our charity. Every person that we give to is an immortal being created in the image of God; every gift we give, a symbol of his love.

Prayer will call us to action that is death-defying, perilous, and anything but pretty. Lives of prayer are of a substance with the Cross. But we start where we are. God will surely speak to us, make no mistake, but he will use the language of our daily lives. And at each step of the way, we must respond where we are, how we are, sinners saved by splendored grace, wanting only to please him.

Spiritual Direction

Often in books about spiritual formation, readers are encouraged to consider *spiritual direction*, which is really no more or no less than involving another person in your listening to God. Spiritual direction is an ongoing relationship between two people who meet, or perhaps talk by phone, on a regular basis for the purpose of one Christian being helped by another to become more attuned to God's presence and to respond more fully to that presence in daily life. When these two people meet or talk, the director and directee seek to enter into a prayerful atmosphere where together they can be attentive to the Holy Spirit. The director will prayerfully listen, and occasionally ask questions, as directed by God's Spirit. Quite simply, the director is a facilitator who creates an environment of listening to God and opening to grace. While therapy and counseling deal primarily with problems in one's life and attempts to find healthy solutions, spiritual direction is concerned with finding and responding to God. A natural inclination is to jump in and be helpful; a spiritual director squelches this impulse, which can interfere with God's working in our lives.

At some point in my new prayer venture, when I began to feel the need for input from outside the narrow boundaries of my brain, I decided to look for a spiritual director. No simple search, this. The truth is, my hometown of Northampton, Massachusetts, is not exactly overrun with resources for the Christian pilgrim. When I introduce myself to Christians in other parts of the United States, the response is often, "Ah, Northampton: Jonathan Edwards," as though the sainted prophet still rides his horse down Main Street. In point of fact, were Edwards preaching here this Sunday, his service would be one many offerings: from Baha'i to Buddhist, from pantheist to Wiccan. In my hometown, where beings such as I are considered anomalous, if not downright quaint, spiritual direction can be hard to find.

However, some serious detective work, enabled by the very grace of God, put me in touch with a spiritual director who lived an hour's drive from home. This pastor sounded fairly excellent. One teeny-tiny glitch: he was off to South Africa and wouldn't be available for a number of months. Fast-forward two years. I am cleaning out my saved e-mails—a practice good for both mind *and* soul—and I stumble on this pastor's contact information. I fire off a query to him, asking clearly if he might help me listen to God's speaking, and a week later we meet for the first time. We've chosen to meet in a public building halfway between our two towns, and while we stand on the chilly sidewalk waiting for the building to open, this man, whom I will call Andrew, stands at some remove from the small group of waiting people. I glance over, and I see that he is praying. He looks so attentive and so focused. When you meet with someone who you hope will help you pray, this is a most encouraging sign.

In fact, it reminded me of a theology conference I had attended at Wheaton College, where one of my top favorite theologians was a featured speaker. (He shall be nameless, as I am a major fan of privacy, and I like to think the people I admire the most—at least those still walking on the earth— are too.) Before the evening session I was prowling the tables outside, those groaning boards weighed down by piles of books that make a lifetime seem even shorter than originally advertised. I spotted the speaker at the far corner of the sales table and slowly made my way in his direction, without any agenda beyond perhaps a brilliant, life-changing conversation. As I moved closer, I could hear the singing of an old familiar hymn. Perhaps it was "What a Friend We Have in

Jesus." Perhaps it was "The Old Rugged Cross." This man, this writer and thinker and teacher, was singing—softly for sure, and to himself for certain, but singing nonetheless. But he showed no awareness of his song. He seemed so clearly to be listening, to be attending with obvious concentration.

I learned something that day: you can't approach a singing person. I don't know why, but you can't interrupt, not even if the singing person is famous, not even if he is brilliant and one of your favorite writers. I was miffed. *How unavailable!* I thought. *How self-contained. People at book tables should be open to chat; a small hello, at least.*

I went inside the auditorium and sat down. This brilliant theologian, this bookstall crooner, spoke that night about God; about putting God first; about creating a place, and space, and time for worship and communion with our Savior, no matter where we are, no matter what's going on around us. He spoke of not only speaking *to* God, but also listening, tuning in to God and to his speaking, even when surrounded by competing voices. Standing by the books, I had seen this man worshiping, in his heart and in his whispered songs, as though he were alone with God.

These praying men bring home one point to me; that is, if we are to be helped in our lives of prayer by other people, let those people be the ones who pray, the ones who have learned what it means to listen to the Lord, to hear his voice. I'm here to say that no matter how much time we pray, there are hours in the day that we all spend with other people, and

I think we could make a pretty strong case that it matters who those people are. I think in every life, one priority is finding one or more seasoned Christians with whom to spend some serious time.

I think our spiritual directors, our mentors in a life of faith—whether they be those we meet in person or those whose books we read—must be people whose lives radiate the magnificent splendor of close communion with our God.

I walked into an open church one weekday afternoon with my spiritual director, Andrew. On that late autumn day, the wind was blowing forcefully, the temperatures hinting at the New England winter's coming attractions.

"Wow," Andrew said as we stepped inside. "Listen."

"What?" I said.

"God," Andrew replied, and shook his head in frank amazement. "He is so beautiful."

Andrew takes God's word seriously. He thinks if the Bible says, "Pray without ceasing" (1 Thessalonians 5:17 KJV), it probably means, *Pray without ceasing*. He helps me learn to listen and to pray, and he lives a life suffused with prayer. There is great power in knowing when we sit, or stand, or kneel at home to pray alone, that others in our lives are praying too.

And Andrew also takes seriously other biblical instructions, such as: "Rejoice always" (1 Thessalonians 5:16). He's the only person I know who always brings to mind two particular words: *mirth* and *merry*—*merry*-ness being a quality I have so very frequently observed in monastics. It must be an

119

occupational hazard for those who hear the one voice we so often fail to listen for.

But what's all this got to do with our private lives of prayer? A lot, I think. We are formed by our surroundings. We are made comfortable when we see others doing that which makes us feel a little shy. I feel silly standing in the middle of my backyard on a gray November day, singing "Be Still My Soul" within earshot of nobody but the squirrels and blackbirds, until, that is, I think of standing by the endless piles of books at Wheaton College, hearing those soft songs to Jesus sung in earnest praise.

Having a spiritual director is a God-blessed opportunity to speak of prayer aloud. In one of our first meetings, I re-member telling Andrew that keeping my mind on God was a real challenge for me, even in the middle of my prayers. He suggested that I totally focus in on God, in order to listen to his voice, during the three minutes in which the coffeemaker does its thing in my early-morning kitchen. I didn't like that advice. I didn't want to focus on God for a minute. I wanted a challenge; I wanted to start with an hour and progress from there. It took me months before I followed his suggestion, but when I finally did, I realized there is something qualita-tively different in having this laser focus, even for the very briefest time, much as if you stop the world for a minute, get off, and kneel down to gaze into the eyes of a child. There's dynamite contained within that tiny particle of time; there is transport, liminal awareness, all in a heartbeat.

Private prayer is private, and it is individual and something that we do alone, but other Christians can help us learn to pray, in concrete and specific ways. For anyone who might like to explore finding a spiritual director, it is first and foremost important to ask God's guidance in the search. There may be a person already known to you with whom you might begin to have this special relationship, as a spiritual director may have formal training or may have natural gifts for this ministry. Many websites offer listings of Christians who offer spiritual direction, as do retreat centers, religious communities, and centers that train spiritual directors. In this search, as in all aspects of our lives, we must always be attentive to the leading of the Holy Spirit.

Spiritual direction is a relationship like no other. It is a place where the life and well-being of the soul receive attentive care, where the *eternal* merits concentrated focus, and where God is sought and found. A spiritual director understands what it means to be used as an instrument of grace, to be one who doesn't speak so much as listen, giving prayerful attentiveness to those he helps and to their Heavenly Father.

Chapter Eight
WHAT'S THEOLOGY GOT TO DO WITH IT?

IN THE COURSE OF MY FOUR-TIMES-A-DAY discipline, I have sometimes found myself asking, *What is my theology of prayer?* That is, what do I believe about the nature of the practice and the One to whom I pray?

Much of this may seem obvious, but it is important to say clearly that prayer does not exist as a freestanding endeavor; the practice cannot be divorced from the One to whom our prayers are addressed. And surely all prayers are addressed, sealed, stamped, and sent somewhere, and so they will be deeply influenced by our understanding of the *recipient*, be that God, or nature, or art, or the universe, or the spirit within. This is a concept of both magnitude and consequence, a matter that we need to consider if we are to pray and live in satisfying communion with the Lord God.

The Knowledge of the Holy

The book *The Knowledge of the Holy*, by A. W. Tozer, is probably the one piece of writing, apart from Scripture, that has had the most profound influence on my life. For decades, it has been the book I reread each year during Lent, and some years in other seasons as well. In this small but profound exposition, Tozer sets himself the task of writing about the attributes of God: God as independent, omnipotent, loving, faithful, and truly other. Tozer teases out the reverberations of each attribute as he offers help to understand and experience each one as it plays out in our lives. He contends that every human problem is theological, and he makes a case that will convince even the most skeptical of the wisdom of these words. The book is dated now, its references and language of another time and sensibility, but every sentence in the book rewards the reader. On the final page, Tozer concludes with four words of advice: "Acquaint thyself with God."

If this is not the business of our prayers, then I don't know what is. Here is the stark antithesis of prayer for prayer's sake. Here lies the reason that we might do well to analyze our theology of prayer, comparing it to prayers of our friends who pray to art, to the universe, or to goodwill. We are wasting our lifetimes if we fail to study, to ponder, and to seriously consider *to whom* we pray, and based upon that understanding, *how* we pray to him.

Acquaint thyself with God.
It is our starting place.
It is our destination.

He Is the Lord

If prayer matters, and if we even consider that it is something we might attempt with daily discipline and care, then we will do well to invest a bit of time and thought considering its most elementary foundation.

There will be no shortage of big questions: *Who is God? What is he like?* And, *Who am I? What might be the nature of communication between us?* And surely, ours will be a theology that evolves across the span of what will be a lifetime.

Speaking for myself, I think that almost every time God shows up in a sentence that I speak about him, he nearly drowns, weighted by the millstones of my myths and misconceptions. I say I want to know about God, but I sometimes wonder if I want to know God as he is or if I am in the market for a God I can dress up and take to church, a God who will not bewilder or embarrass me, a God who never threatens me with love designed to utterly transform my very life.

We know how frail and tenuous we are. We sense our frailty every time we trip over a raised brick in the sidewalk; every time we get a diagnosis that comes wrapped up in a package with an expiration date; every time we get any bad news—never in short supply. When we witness how easily a life can suddenly end, we sometimes feel we are constructed out of tissue paper, curling tape, and rubber bands. In these moments we get glimmers of the miracle it is that any life goes on from day to day.

By God's grace, somewhere deep inside we realize God is God. This doesn't always strike us as good news. In the first place, it brings us face-to-face with our inadequacy. In our sincere prayers we are confronted by the frailty we spend so much energy denying. And, in the second place, we know that if God ever rescues us, we'll die. That's the plan. It's stated clearly in the information packet. And if we allow ourselves the honesty to see it, we know that just being in the same town with him could crisp us up to cinders, reduce us to ash with neither memory, form, nor reason. And so, more often than we might admit, we avoid him like the plague—like several plagues, each with its own cotillion of distressing consequences. And what better way to avoid him than to draw near, to know where he is and what he's up to, to keep him in sight at all times, and to pray in ways that make it very clear that we are happy to have God join in to whatever scheme we have in mind, to bless and keep us, but requiring that he keep a low profile all the same.

Does Prayer Work?

I am asked with some regularity, "Does prayer work?"

"Oh yes. Big time," I always want to answer. "Prayer gives us communion, relationship, experience of God in Christ through the Holy Spirit, the means of grace, and the hope of glory."

But I know full well that answer might betray a misunderstanding of the question.

"Does prayer produce desired results?" is what is being asked, I think.

And if that is the question, my answer would be, "Hardly ever," or hardly ever in a way that we intend. Prayer definitely changes something, and that something is most often *the person who is praying*. Prayer changes *us* in ways beyond our own designing. That is, I think, one of the reasons I might be inclined to limit my praying, and why I resist the kind of prayer that leaves me open to the working of God in my life. Sometimes I think that prayer is the opposite of being in control, and who wants that! Thinking through our theology of prayer will help us see more clearly our resistance to the enterprise. I know full well that I resist prayer, in subtle or more forthright ways, often with prayers that don't give God much of an opening in the conversation.

We can have a theology of praying, and just as truly, we can have a theology of *not* praying. I think it might run something like this: "Truth be told, I don't pray much, but I am a Christian. I love Jesus, I go to church, and I try to live a good life, so therefore God must be Someone who doesn't really care whether I pray or not. To him, it must be optional. I should pray more, but bottom line, I think God's fine with my not praying."

For most of my life, that is how my functioning theology has played out in practice. Oh, I might sit every morning for an hour, gearing up to pray. I read Scripture; I read books. I had ten or twelve great books at all times stacked beside my praying chair. But most days I was lucky if five minutes of that hour I did in fact pray. I was like the wife who reads a million books on how to have a world-class marriage but six nights a week skips dinner with her husband.

My functional theology of prayer has been: it's optional. As in so many areas of theology, the doctrine I espoused was founded not on Scripture, not on the teachings of the church, but on the particulars of my own behavior. Many contemporary decisions regarding morality follow just this creative logic: we watch what we do, and we decide it is good because we do it. We do not pray, and upon the basis of that behavior, we decide it is OK.

But God is Lord of all, or he is not Lord at all. Christianity is many things, but one thing it is not is a sideline, a nice hobby, a part-time occupation. We have two choices: in or out; holy or not holy. We must never pretend God sent his Son to die so that we might have life occasionally, so that we might flicker in and out.

Abide, he says.

In me.

In our minds and hearts, we will live on the mountaintop, or we will discover in the end that we have lived our lives, always, every day, and more and more with passing time, slowly sinking into the murky swampland below.

If all day, every day, we are meant to be abiding, working,

and resting in our Savior, with every thought and impulse trained on him, then we need to live where that is not only likely, but also possible. If our inner, spiritual life is meant to be lived on a mountain, communing day and night with the Lord God, and if we spend twenty-three hours and forty-five minutes a day in something that can feel like a swirling swampland below, we might just have a problem. Caught up in the preoccupation of making lives amid the tangling grasses in the murky water, with our *spiritual* life consisting of ascending the mountain once a day for fifteen minutes to "be with God," we are surely orchestrating failure.

Holy living, discipline, and abstinence are all old-fashioned terms. I think a sinful world has gradually conditioned the Christian, wooed and lulled her into an unthinking acceptance of so much that is worldly and worthless, hammering at her senses, battering out of existence needed sensitivity. Our lives are destroying the opportunity for silence, where the soul might hear the still small voice of God; our habits are killing off even our ability to sit down all alone with nothing—with everything—with a Holy God.

The problem is that the *screens* in our lives—the media that teach and train and mold us, the screens through which we view the world—erode our expectations, changing our values, standards, and perspectives without our awareness or conscious consent.

Prayer is not something we do in a vacuum. Prayer is affected by the hours in the day when we aren't praying. The mountain where we want to live isn't easy to attain. In fact, it is impossible, unless God picks us up and transports us there, giving us the choice in our moment-by-moment decisions, to abide, to listen, and to pray; to learn through days and years of worship and of praise what blessing God has for us there. This has to do with

We must make God our habit, till he becomes our dwelling place.

where we live. We must make God our habit, till he becomes our dwelling place. God is not someone we visit.

A theology of prayer that understands prayer as the centerpiece of life will offer no alternative. We are not free to say, "Well, prayer is not really my thing, so I'll do service, feed the poor, give money, fight for justice, teach and preach." Whatever prayer may be, whatever theology of prayer we may espouse, if we are sons and daughters of God in Christ by the Holy Spirit, prayer is not an option we might practice or neglect.

Let us begin with looking heavenward, to see our God; to wonder who and what he is; to make it the business of a lifetime to discover him. And then will follow other questions: Are our prayers grounded in consciousness of God? Or are our prayers primarily focused on ourselves? Do we pray in order to know God better? Or do we pray in order to tell God what we and he already know in great detail about ourselves, our lives, our needs, our wants and wishes, our miseries and dissatisfactions, and the ultimate direction we would like to see things go, failing in the end to know the Lord to whom we pray?

Acquaint thyself with God.

As we attempt to define and live into a biblical theology of prayer, we can get valuable information about the theology we now espouse, from listening to our thoughts while we are actually praying. We need to see our error, if we mean to set things right.

When Mary Magdalene first sees Jesus after the Resurrection, she does not recognize him. The risen Lord stands ready not only to astound her but also to bless her as the first living being to see him risen from the dead, and she lays out her plans for corpse anointment with some potent perfume. There she stands at the empty tomb, telling the risen Lord her plans for his dead body.

I know no clearer picture of many of my prayers. God is alive and well and standing by the window in my sunroom, fully prepared to blow the morning wide open with his newly minted mercies, his splendor, and his love; and I sit, bathrobed and blanketed, sipping tepid tea, telling him how I intend to get on with my day. Oh, I don't spell out my theology of prayer, not in so many words. But what I do is I begin to pray, "Our father who art in heaven," and by the time I've gotten to "Thy kingdom come," in my mind I'm standing in line at Best Buy rehearsing how I'll get the Geek Squad to best serve my needs; and before I've reached "Thy will be done," I'm single-handedly settling the dispute about computer repairs with the express intention of *my own* will not just being done, but also being thought well of by everybody else in line.

I dismiss all this by saying my mind wanders, as though it had gone off on some harmless ramble, while in point of fact my mind went off to devise my plans for getting on with life without a risen Savior. Prayer is a chance to see our thoughts for what they are, to understand how they portray our theology of prayer. Before we can let the mind of Christ be in us, we must first see the minds we already have and become familiar with their wily ways. We are told to "capture every thought to make it obedient to Christ" (2 Corinthians 10:5). Could that mean even when we are praying?

My prayers sometimes sound like this: "Our father who art in heaven," *there's that shoulder pain again. I wonder if I'll need surgery. I shouldn't take so many aspirin. Should I see a specialist?* "Give us this day our daily bread." *If Tony gets promoted, I can't work under him. He's such a nasty human being. I'll need a new job.* "Lead us not into temptation." *Darn, I forgot to defrost the chicken, and I have to pay Andrea back. I hate obligation. She's too demanding as it is* . . . "the kingdom, and the power, and the glory. Amen."

My prayer could be so different. It could be like this: "Our father who art in heaven," *there's that shoulder pain again. Please heal me as you will or won't, but give me grace sufficient.* "Hallowed be thy name. Thy kingdom come. Thy will be done." *If Tony gets promoted, God, I do not like that man. I do not know why; but I believe that you have known him from before he was created, and you love him, and you died for him, and I pray that I could see him with those eyes* . . . "on earth as it is in heaven. Give us this day our daily bread." *Oh Lord, I forgot to defrost the chicken. I am a dyed-in-the-wool Martha caring about so many things. Please give me a quiet, settled spirit, I pray in your holy name, and* "forgive us our sins as we forgive those who sin against us." *I want to be so resentful toward my friend Andrea. Please* "deliver me from temptation and lead me not into evil, for thine is the kingdom." *Help me to know what the Kingdom is. Help me to be on fire for your Holy Kingdom all day long,* "and the power." *Please may I know that the power that works in me today is the same power that raised Jesus Christ from the dead* "and the glory." *Glory, glory, glory, hallelujah!* "Amen."

For good or ill, our minds will go off on their rambles. It's how our minds work, one thought leading to another with no scheme or pattern. And it is important to follow these thoughts and see just where they're taking us today. There is much to learn by observing all the places our thoughts would have us go. Many meditation practices endorse observing passing thoughts and daydreams, paying close attention to the messages they bring.

Our wandering thoughts can easily espouse a theology that contradicts our spoken prayers. We are praying for God's will at the very moment we are making plans to exercise our own. We pray for God's help even as we devise plans to carry on and accomplish our goals without him.

Our minds will wander. It's what minds do. But we can "capture every thought to make it obedient to Christ" if we pay attention, if we *attend* to the nature of our thinking, and turn each idea into a prayer for grace, each passing thought into an occasion for thanksgiving.

The word *theology* might strike us as a bit weighty, but whatever we call it, the truth of the matter is that we pretty much have a theology for everything we do. We seldom try to reduce it to words, but if we watch our thoughts, and speech, and actions, we can discover what that theology might be. This discovery can move us to the next step, to an exploration of the theology of prayer that God desires for us to believe and live.

Chapter Nine
EFFECTUAL PRAYER

THERE IS A Q&A I LIKE that references the biblical story of Jacob, later named Israel, the man who wrestles all night with an angel.

The question: How do you know if a man has been with God?

The answer: He limps.

Similarly, another question: How do you know if someone builds his life around prayer?

My answer: His life may look a little odd. (I am a big fan of understatement.)

Make no mistake, instituting four times of prayer—spending time in communion with the Lord—each day will change the fabric and appearance of our days. They will not look the same. They will not be the same. *We* will not be the same.

The Surrounding Hours

The disciplines we commit to do not exist in a vacuum. Our individual practices are part of the larger pattern of our lives. We cannot institute independent disciplines unless they are supported, or at the very least not interfered with, by the rest of what we do. If we want to introduce elements of discipline into a life, they cannot be superimposed as random, isolated insertions. I found that a new prayer practice required far more readjustment than just the clearing of four twenty-minute blocks of time each day. The new schedule actually shifted mealtimes, bedtimes, and hours of rising.

If we confine our prayers to once a day, it is far easier for us to keep intact the boundaries between praying and living. Instituting several distinct prayer times each day promises to change our lives, sometimes in surprising ways. For certain, our hearts are likely to be changed, but also, it is entirely possible that our schedules will be different, our priorities upended, our ways of moving through a day now responding to divine rhythms. Let us never think that being with our God will only change us inside. Our lives will bear the mark; our schedules and date books will sport the imprint of Another's hand.

And, if we spend four times a day in worship and communion, the hours when we are not actively at prayer will be newly branded, a prayer-like state will pervade our common ways.

I Want to Be Alone

Prayer changes our lives, but prayer is not a self-improvement project. (Thank God!) Prayer is the way we come into correspondence with our design, our intended *individual* and *corporate* design. God did not create us, nor did God redeem us, in order to make little freestanding Christians, autonomous and unrelated. We are made to be part of one Body, one Church, one Bride.

Sadly, I have heard friends describe their blessed, holy, sacred private times with God but then add that they are really not "into" church or community with other Christians. These folks *pray* often and most devoutly but disregard the people they are called not just to like but to love—and love with a life-giving, death-willing devotion. The primary *effect* of prayer is to bring us into actual, observable, holy communion and relationship with God, Father, Son, and Holy Spirit, and with *the people* who make up the church, in service to God's world. It's a package deal. We don't get God without his family. There can be a certain pernicious temptation in prayer to make it all about him and me. (Do I hear echoes born in sibling rivalry?)

It's easy to find God in nature, in serving the poor, and in the commonplace—but God can be a bit elusive in a church. Church: this attempt to put people and God into the same auditorium for at least an hour every Sunday morning. People: the tricky part. I remember vividly a day of deepest full-of-glory adoration of my Savior. I went to church that evening, walked in, sat down, and my first thought was, *Dear God, I cannot believe you like these people.*

I find it easiest to be together in morning worship as we sit with coats still on, kneeling, rising, reading, touching lips and sternums, turning bodies ninety-two degrees to face the huge red book the glassy-eyed teenager carries aloft down the center aisle. My pastor takes her shoes off to preach about a God who talks to her at 5 a.m. out in her barn. A baby cries, gearing up to be the church in this place when we are all dead and gone. Bank checks are tucked in tiny envelopes, placed on a metal plate that a white-robed science teacher will lift skyward at the altar. Songs, none written after the War of 1812, are sung heartily enough above a fractious organ. A man gets tears in his eyes at the words of a Creed he could recite if he were dead, a thing he plans in fact to do.

But, it gets a bit tricky at Bible study, where folks get to speak, and trickier still at committee meetings, where opinions are not always left at the door. Then we travel far, far beyond the outer reaches of the complicated when we try our hand at daily life together. Prayer brings us closer in love to God *and* one another, or it is not prayer.

Prayer teaches us the nature of relationship with both God and all the people in our lives. There is so much that we can learn no other way. On the way to the cross, Jesus asks his Father that his children may love one another as the Father and the Son love. Every prayer takes place in the presence of the Trinity, in the realm of love the Three Persons have from all eternity for one another.

To See God Everywhere in Everything

Prayer unites us to God and to his people, and prayer helps us understand the agency of God in our lives, his

We discover the more we pray, that when unexpected things happen, we find ourselves intrigued, even excited, to see how God is going to work things out for his glory.

presence and his work in circumstance and timing. Life becomes more interesting. We discover the more we pray, that when unexpected things happen, we find ourselves intrigued, even excited, to see how God is going to work things out for his glory. Through prayer, our frame of reference is altered, and every occurrence, every single thing that doesn't go according to plan, is evidence to us that God is at work in our lives. We usually tend to attribute good happenings to God's intervention, and in doing so we can miss a lot, I think. Prayer helps us see God in the upsets and the setbacks; in the small annoyances; in the frank catastrophe.

Another fallout from a life of prayer is that I define myself less by who I am and more by who God is. I realize that my life is all about God in Christ. When I am in communion with my Savior, my emotional health is affected. (I would say that I am not quite so crazy, but then I am not exactly an impartial judge here.) I find I am no longer hiding from God, and so I am no longer hiding from myself, not threatened by my thoughts and feelings. I think very often we are afraid of what we will learn in silence, but as we sit in prayer we realize that we are truly not alone, and this transforms both us and the experience.

Being consciously in God's presence four times a day makes me more conscious of God through all the hours when I am not consciously praying. I find it easier to see his frame of reference. Familiarity breeds acquaintanceship—it really does.

We will find that just the effort to pray is very instructive in itself. When we try to be good, we see exactly how bad we are. When we narrow the channels in our lives, in the sense that we impose certain boundaries on time and activity, this heightened focus means we bump more often into the sides, the constraints, and these often serve as wonderful correctives. It truly is a holding environment, a space in which to "live, and move, and have our being" (Acts 17:28 KJV).

In the end, instead of feeling more confined, we feel only more expansive and free. This freedom comes from living with restraints conforming to our nature. A little boy is given goldfish in a bowl but wants his fish to be free, and so he scoops them up and puts them on the floor, where they can play unimpeded by the glass container. We are no wiser than he, confusing freedom with a lack of limits. The discipline of regular praying times frees us to fit with our design and know the harmony of living as we have been created to live.

Hard Evidence Abounds

When we lead lives of prayer, the way we do our lives says to those around us that God is different from what they had imagined. Those who know us will see some difference in the way we conduct our lives and move through our days, and from this will see more of the nature of the God we worship. *Christ in me* knows how to do my life far better than I ever could conceive on my own. I am truly changed. Brain scientists tell us that being looked at in love actually affects brain development. It's how we are designed. As we spend time with God, we experience the presence of the Holy Spirit in new and changing ways, learning that his power is beyond anything in our experience.

We become people who live in a new dimension. We are given such a vision that we move toward a place where we will pay any price to know God. I tremble as I write these words because we are entering the territory far beyond our knowledge, control, or conception. If God is truly God, we are dealing with life beyond anything we could ever come up with. I find this both intriguing and appropriately terrifying, but the more I pray, the more I come to know a God whose fierce justice is tempered with heartbreaking mercy.

In prayer we become more and more of what we each personally were intended to be. On the resurrection morning, God will not ask you why you were not Paul. He will ask you why you were not you. In prayer we will be the selves we truly are, bringing in our ideas and perspectives, our memories and imaginings. I believe that each particular imagination is a gift from God. In times of trouble I sometimes envision Christ holding my hand—a very good association for me, reminiscent of my father holding my hand when I was a young child—and loving me. When God feels too abstract, the use of imagination will allow me to reach out and grab this hand, so warm and strong. For every one of us, the images will be particular ones that touch our hearts most truly, and they may well be different for each of us.

Much is being written at this cultural moment to suggest that God is the product of our imaginings rather than their source, that, in fact, he is created in the workshops of our minds. I might find these ideas a bit more compelling if this God—the one I am encouraged to understand as a whimsical creation of my magnificent imagination—had not spent so much face time in the Middle East, leaving such a pesky trail of witnesses whose reports loom large and so relentlessly persistent across millennia.

A Point of View

Prayer offers us a new point of reference. We listen to the evening news and know that we commune with the One who is in fact running the whole show. His presence and the knowledge of his power make it hard for us to get very nervous. Christ is not holding just my hand; he is holding the fate of the universe.

The more time we spend in prayer, the more we experience the love of God; the more we feel the Father looking at us as his beloved child, the more we grow and become like his Son. The *mind of Christ* cannot be in me if I don't know what it is, but if he is beside me all day long and if I am repeatedly turning my thoughts to him, I have an increasingly clear idea of that mind of my Savior.

Feeling Feelings

There is the experience of love and beauty in the communion with God that we are offered in prayer. Two teenagers newly fallen into love sit in a room full of people who barely register on their radar, their rapt attention held only by one another. There are valid criticisms of the practice of romanticizing the relationship of the Christian and God, but at the other extreme we miss a great deal when we fail to understand the nature of love between a soul and the Savior. One has only to read the great mystics through the ages, whose lives have been consumed by prayer, to see that what we call romance is indeed a part of what we understand as love. Prayer gives us a greater experience of love than anything else in life. Prayer involves every aspect of who and what we are; not the least of that is emotion.

We know how warm and wonderful feeling can be, how captivating and pervading, blessing and enlivening. Love and emotion will be our common experience in what it is we have with God. All good feeling comes from God the Creator, part and parcel of the whole arrangement in the first place. We strip God of his majesty when we leave emotion out of our worship and substitute instead some wooden form of our own inventing.

Prayer changes my response to things. When I wake up ill at 3 a.m., I find I do not cry out, "God help me; God help me," as once was my custom. Rather, I find myself turning over and whispering in the cold night air, "Well, Lord, you know what this is, and thank you for being with me here and taking care of this in the way that will be for the very best." Praying will beget new prayers.

When troubled thoughts—worry, anxiety, concern, or obsession—arrive to set up shop inside my addled brain, they won't be driven out without some stronger, more compelling replacement. The more I steep my soul in prayer, the more the image of the Lord God Almighty strikes me with a force and beauty that makes all other thinking pretty puny, flimsy, weak, and silly. The more I spend my life in conscious devotion, the more the sweetness of the Lord Jesus blasts other thoughts away. To have ideas and ruminations that have troubled me for oh so long give way to the power and the glory of images of God is a gift I treasure.

And so the cycle swirls. God blesses, healing our very thoughts and feelings, and we praise him. We praise him and the adoration moves us closer to his heart. Whatever path we choose to walk in life will take us closer to one destination or another. *This* path takes us closer to home; closer to our God; closer to ourselves as were created and long to be.

So many people live life far from God but imagine heaven at their life's ending. But what a strange state to attain if we are not schooled in worship, practiced in loving praise. What an odd and foreign end that would be.

Longings of My Heart

Prayer changes our daily habits, our use of time, and our ways of being in relationship with other people and our work as we discover deep-heart, thoughtful connectivity with our lives. Grace is not a reward for good behavior. We don't earn our salvation any more than we chalk up points to obtain mercy. The gracious, munificent goodness of God is unmerited favor. Unmerited. Not deserved. The blessings of prayer are freely given gifts, and it is this fact that changes the way we interact with everybody in our lives. It is our experience of being on the receiving end that fashions how we give.

And finally, prayer allows us to acknowledge and attend to the deepest longings of our hearts. We find out what they are, what they tell us about who *we* are, and how they will one day all be met in him.

We spend so much of our lives standing at a distance from our longing.
Prayer brings us close, where longings live.

I write short stories—that's my day job—and I find writing fiction is a great way to discover what my own heart longs for. It is winter—imagine cold, gray, fading daylight; black night beginning to fall before the afternoon is done—and I am writing a story about a very old woman who is dying. This character lies in and out of consciousness, sometimes confusing people in the room with her loved ones, dead and gone for time out of mind. At one point she sees her father standing there; she feels him take her small child's hand in his.

"Will you be with me when I die?" she says. "Will you hold my hand?"

"Of course" is his reply.

They move the aged woman to a hospice center. She sees her father through the window, running along beside the ambulance that carries her to the last place she will ever be. Once settled in her room, she sees her father there again.

"I'm not afraid to die," she says. He takes her hand.

We spend so much of our lives standing at a distance from our longing.

Prayer brings us close, where longings live, where our dreams meet grace.

Chapter Ten
ZACHEUS AND TEA PARTIES

.

IN THE GOSPELS, WHEN JESUS SAYS, "Come unto me," there are a lot of pretty sweet words attached to the invitation: *rest, gentle, humble heart, easy,* and *light.* But there are also a couple of words that aren't quite as winsome: *yoke* and *burden.* What's up with that? If you're inviting people to follow you, those might not be the two top words to seal the deal. Come unto me and I will give you a yoke and a burden. *Easy and light. Yoke and burden.*

Life is easy. And life is very hard. And we know very well some of the worst burdens in life are all about the struggles that we have inside, the ones nobody sees.

"Come unto me. . . . For my yoke is easy, and my burden is light," Jesus says (Matthew 11:28-30 KJV).

This is the same Jesus who bids us come and die, who says, "Take up [your] cross daily, and follow me" (Luke 9:23).

So what's with this *easy yoke* business? What's this about lightweight burdens? And what's it got to do with prayer?

I think marriage can help us understand. Two people,

often two very *young* people, get all dressed up, stand up in public, and sign up for a yoke—a burden, one that involves promises about whom they will and will not love, and what they will and will not do, for *as long as they both shall live.* Years ago a friend gave me his definition of marriage. He told me marriage was a promise that at the moment in the future when what you wanted more than anything in the world was to walk away, you would stick around. I thought that was awful. "Where's the romance?" I asked him. Now, I think it's one of the most romantic things I've ever heard. This kind of taking of a yoke is based on love, not gushy, mushy hormones. It's based upon the understanding that by giving up certain so-called freedoms, you enter a relationship with rights and privileges and joys you cannot know any other way. It is the assuming of a yoke not just designed for you but one you were designed to wear.

And the taking of this yoke comes from love—mutual love. For a lot of years I didn't know what it meant to love God, not really. And finally—I'm a slow, slow learner—I asked God to give me love for him. I prayed that he would give me the love for himself. I couldn't even do that on my own. And he answered that prayer, the prayer that the yoke and burden would be fashioned out of love.

Come unto Me. Take My Yoke.

So where do we sign up for this yoke we were designed for?

We sign up at the cross. We reach the place of peace, and ease, and gentle sweetness at the point of crucifixion; the crucifixion of our Savior, God; the crucifixion of ourselves when we sign up—when we sign up every morning, and in our new discipline of prayer, when we sign up every noon, and every suppertime, and every evening.

What we're in the market for is peace and pleasant things. And what we're offered is peace "which surpasses all understanding" (Philippians 4:7 NKJV), peace the world can neither give nor take away, and not just pleasantness but "joy unspeakable and full of glory" (1 Peter 1:8 KJV).

Jesus says, "Come unto me," but I think more often our lives say to Jesus, "You come unto me." We pray and our prayers say in effect, "Dear Lord, here's what I'm going to do. Please bless it. Here's my plan. I'd love to have you join me."

We sing, "Come, thou fount of every blessing," when usually it's the thirsty man who comes to the fountain and not the other way around. "Come, thou almighty King," we sing, when typically it's not the king who makes home visits.

Don't get me wrong. I am not faulting the theology of the hymns we sing. They've got it dead right. We can come to Jesus for one reason and one alone, and that is because he comes to us, God drawing our hearts to him. God reveals himself to us.

So let me ask a question. Are we experiencing our lives in Christ as yokes so easy, burdens so light? And how do we move and grow to a place where that is more often the case?

Jesus doesn't say, "Come over here and let me put this yoke on you; let me harness you up." He says, "Take my yoke." He says, "Learn from me."

How do we do it? There's no surprise here; the answer is in prayer.

There is one way to the Father, and that is through the atonement of God's Son. But I also think that there are other aspects of a life in Christ that comprise the yoke we're asked to take.

Throughout the Gospels Jesus is always going off to be alone with his Father. Jesus required that. His heart longed for that. "Take my yoke. Learn from me."

We are offered all of the wealth of the kingdom of God, all of the dynamite dazzle of what it means to live every moment of the day not only in the wild and wooly awareness that the God of Creation knows who we are and where we live, but also on top of that, in the amazement that he wants anything to do with us. I think we would be well advised to spend a whole lot more of our time walking around amazed. We believe the wildest story anyone's telling: that God, the God, is not only real, loving, eternal, and spectacular in every aspect, but that God is interested in coming home with us for lunch this afternoon. We can come to him because he comes to us. I remember a children's song:

I think we would be well advised to spend a whole lot more of our time walking around amazed.

149

Zacheus was a wealthy man, and a wealthy man was he.

He climbed up in a sycamore tree and there the Lord to see.

And when the Lord was passing by he looked up in that tree.

And he said, "Zacheus, you come down for I'm going to your house for tea."

God is magnificent, unapproachable, holy, and almighty. We can't reach him. But he has come to us so we can come to him. He has taken on himself the yoke that crushed the world, the cross that if we had to bear would destroy us, so that we can take the yoke we were designed to wear.

"Come unto me."

And when we start to move in that direction, he's right there.

We spend a lot of our lives like Zacheus, up in trees trying to get a peek at Jesus, when what Jesus is saying is, "Get down here. I'm going to your house for tea."

Appendix

GROUP CONTEMPLATIVE
PRAYER: AN AID
TO PRIVATE PRAYER

E VERY PRAYER WE PRAY—EVERY BREATH WE TAKE, come
to that—constitutes experience of the triune God, the
Three Persons of the Trinity, eternally in loving relationship before the world began. That we serve a triune God—
a God who is in, and indeed is, community—has major
implications for our prayer in community. As we move
toward a life in which we pray four times a day, we should
include prayer gatherings with other people as part of our
practice. Every prayer life is made better by fellowship with
others.

There is a growing interest in contemplative prayer, an
ancient practice of the church, which takes various forms involving quieting the mind, sitting in silence, opening to God,
and letting go of any agenda or expectation. This can be a
wonderful aid to our individual prayers in communion with

God. In the simplest terms, contemplative prayer—in fact, all prayer—is not something we do; it is something God does, blessing us in relationship with him. Contemplative prayer practice helps us put ourselves in the place where that blessing is conscious and immediate.

Small groups are a great way to develop a practice of contemplative prayer, and what is offered here is a specific format utilizing e-mail as a primary tool. It is designed for a group with little or no experience in this form of prayer.

Ideally six or seven people, who are at least curious and interested, get together for an initial meeting. All members will need to be present at this meeting, which will offer an introduction to basic concepts and to the other members of the group. Following this, on Sunday afternoon of each week for six weeks, one member of the group will send out the e-mail designated below for that particular week. On Friday of each week, this person will send the Friday e-mail below asking for feedback from each member on his or her contemplative practice during the week.

INITIAL MEETING:

At this meeting, the leader will explain that in essence contemplative prayer is listening to God. The leader might stress the following:

> ❧ There is no right or wrong way to do this, no formula or requirements.

❦ It may feel quite different from prayers where we do the talking.

❦ This is a way of spending time with God in fellowship, in silence. There is no agenda.

After a brief introduction, members will be asked to introduce themselves, sharing hopes and longings for the weeks ahead and saying anything about current prayer practices that they might wish to share. For the next portion of the time together, the leader will ask members to sit comfortably and silently with eyes closed as he or she reads a short portion of Scripture, allowing silences in between each of three repetitions of the passage, and asking each time, "What is God saying to you in this passage?" Then each member will share very briefly his or her experience of the listening session.

At the conclusion of this meeting, the leader will explain the following format: each Sunday, members will receive an instruction e-mail detailing an exercise to be completed during the coming week. Each Friday, members will be encouraged to send an e-mail to the group, sharing very briefly their experiences with the exercise for that week. Members will need to give permission to receive one e-mail from each member each week, and all will understand these to be confidential communications. At the end of six weeks, the group will hold a final meeting to share in person the experience of the contemplative practice. The concluding meeting should be scheduled at the time of the first meeting, both for convenience and also for framing the course of the contemplative experience.

The exercises that follow may seem very simple, but we don't start a practice of contemplative prayer with a ten-day silent retreat—though fair warning: we may end up there. This kind of prayer is such sweet blessing that we long for more and more. The format offered here purposely avoids direction to websites and online resources—with one notable exception—because these might so easily be used as substitutes for praying. Contemplative prayer is not a program. There are no rules. It is the soul's communion with God, initiated and enabled by the Holy Spirit. The simplicity of the instructions offered below is intentional and designed to foster an understanding of contemplative prayer as orchestrated by God. We can place ourselves in various circumstances, using aids of art and nature and music, but God is God. It is his pleasure to be with us. He shows us the way.

The following are the e-mails to be sent out each Sunday. You may wish to adapt them slightly, but they should be as brief and nondirective as possible.

WEEK ONE:

As we begin this journey together, let us all keep in mind that the exercise for the week is one you must tailor to fit yourself. Each of us will do these differently. For our first week, please find a five-minute block of time and go outdoors. It might be anywhere. The instructions are simple: look up at the sky. Feel the ground beneath your feet. Be aware of the weather, light, darkness, sound, and quiet. Then, naturally turn your thoughts to God. Consider for a moment that the God who made everything that surrounds you also created you, cares for you, and actually wants to be in relationship with you. Allow yourself to just stand still, aware that you are standing in the presence of your God. You only need to do this one time, but if you wish you may try to do it several times during the week, perhaps once a day at different times of the day in different places. But where or when, once or a number of times, simply stand in the presence of your God.

The instructions are simple: look up at the sky. Feel the ground beneath your feet. Be aware of the weather, light, darkness, sound, and quiet. Then, naturally turn your thoughts to God.

WEEK TWO:

Sometime during this next week, set aside five minutes you will spend in some public place. Find a place to sit, allow your thoughts to focus on the presence of God, and then look at the people all around you. Hold the conscious thought as you see one person and then another that this is an eternal being, made by God, loved by God, a soul who is engaged in a spiritual journey. Become aware of God's focus on this individual's life, both in the moment and always. Focus on each person as one who is known by God. Do this as many times during the coming week as you might like.

WEEK THREE:

Sometime during this week, take a few minutes to select a sample of Christian art. You might find this online, in the public library art section, at a local art museum, or in a book you have at home. Set aside five minutes during the week to look at the chosen image. Allow your thoughts to focus on God, who is present with you, and simply look at the image, with no agenda or expectation. Do this once or any number of times during the week.

WEEK FOUR:

Sometime during this week invite another Christian whom you know to sit and pray with you for ten minutes' time. Once you are seated together in a place where you will not be interrupted, spend the ten minutes together, sitting comfortably, eyes closed, in silence. Focus together on the God who is present with you. There is no agenda; you are just spending a few minutes together in the presence of your loving Father.

WEEK FIVE:

Sometime during the coming week, locate a church or cathedral in your town that is open for prayer. Visit this sanctuary at a time when it is empty, and sit quietly with your Lord and Savior. Be aware that you are simply spending a few minutes in the blessing of communion with your God.

WEEK SIX:

This week, pick a selection of Gregorian chant on a CD or from the surprisingly lovely offerings on www.YouTube. com. Pick one evening at a time when you will not be disturbed, light a single candle in a darkened room, and play the chant softly as you stand alone—but so profoundly *not* alone—in the quiet darkness. You might choose to do this exercise a number of times this week, at the close of your day.

E-MAIL TO BE SENT OUT EVERY WEEK ON FRIDAY:

Would you please take a few moments to write down something of your experience with the exercise this week, anything that you would like to share—perhaps a word about the blessing or the strangeness, the difficulty or the ease of the exercise? Please send your response to the others in our contemplative group by pressing *Reply All.*

CONCLUDING MEETING:

The final meeting should begin with a few minutes of silence, to focus on God's presence, together as a group. Each member should be given about ten minutes to share the experience of the past six weeks in any way he or she likes.

The leader should reiterate that one of the most difficult aspects of the introduction to contemplative prayer is coming to the deep understanding that there is no right or wrong way to do this. There is no agenda, beyond our wish to spend time with God. So many of us have been taught that all prayer is talking, so the practice of listening, being still and open to God, will be a new experience. It does feel strange at first.

Part of this concluding meeting will be the group's deciding whether to continue, using any format—be that meeting to practice contemplative prayer as a group or continuing to receive and send weekly e-mails. A fitting end of the gathering will be thankful praise for the beauty of this experience.

NOTES

1. One Pilgrim's Story

"Taste and see how good the LORD is"

> (Psalms 34:8).

When questioned by Martha, Jesus said that her sister Mary had chosen the better part in listening to his teachings.

> See Luke 10:41.

"Jesus would withdraw to deserted places for prayer" (Luke 5:16).

Jesus consistently went off alone to pray to his Father.

> See Matthew 14:23.

"Three times a day he got down on his knees and prayed"

> (Daniel 6:10 NIV).

It was the *third hour* on the day of Pentecost when 120 disciples were in the upper room praying and were filled with the Holy Spirit.

> See Acts 2:3, 15.

"Peter and John went up together . . ."

> (Acts 3:1 KJV).

Peter went up on the housetop to pray at about the *sixth hour* when he saw a vision of a great sheet, full of all kinds of beasts, let down from heaven.

> See Acts 10:9.

"It was nine in the morning when they crucified him"

> (Mark 15:25).

"From noon until three in the afternoon the whole earth was dark"

> (Mark 15:33; Matthew 27:45).

"It was now about noon, and darkness covered the whole earth until about three o'clock"

> (Luke 23:44).

"Brothers and sisters, we have confidence that we can enter the holy of holies by means of Jesus' blood"
> (Hebrews 10:19).

2. Why Prayer?

"Where your treasure is . . ."
> (Matthew 6:21).

"Come now, and let us reason together"
> (Isaiah 1:18 KJV).

"The very hairs of your head . . ."
> (Matthew 10:30 KJV).

"I know the plans I have in mind for you . . ."
> (Jeremiah 29:11).

"Taste and see how good the LORD is"
> (Psalms 34:8).

Paul prayed for healing three times, and God offered him grace instead.
> See 2 Corinthians 12:8-9.

"Thy will be done"
> (Matthew 6:10 KJV).

"I would never sin against the LORD . . ."
> (1 Samuel 12:23).

". . . provoke one another to love and good works"
> (Hebrews 10:24 WEB).

5. The Practices of Prayer

"Consider the ravens"
> (Luke 12:24).

". . .bodies as a living sacrifice that is holy and pleasing to God"
> (Romans 12:1).

". . . temple[s] of the Holy Spirit"
> (1 Corinthians 6:19).

"God be merciful to me a sinner"
> (Luke 18:13 KJV).

"[God's mercies] are new every morning"
> (Lamentations 3:23 KJV).

". . . fearfully and wonderfully made"
> (Psalm 139:14 KJV).

7. Hearing God's Voice

"Here's what I do know . . ."
(John 9:25).
"What shall it profit a man . . ."
(Mark 8:36 KJV).
"[His] spirit shall not always strive . . ."
(Genesis 6:3 KJV).
"Grieve not the holy Spirit"
(Ephesians 4:30 KJV).
"Pray without ceasing"
(1 Thessalonians 5:17 KJV).
"Rejoice always"
(1 Thessalonians 5:16).

8. What's Theology Got to Do with It?

". . . capture every thought to make it obedient to Christ"
(2 Corinthians 10:5).

9. Effectual Prayer

". . . live, and move, and have our being"
(Acts 17:28 KJV).

10. Zacheus and Tea Parties

"Come unto me. . . ."
(Matthew 11:28-30 KJV).
"Take up [your] cross . . ."
(Luke 9:23).
". . . which surpasses all understanding"
(Philippians 4:7 NKJV).
". . . joy unspeakable and full of glory"
(1 Peter 1:8 KJV).

ACKNOWLEDGMENTS

My thanks to John and Wendy Wilson, who first introduced me to Lil Copan, without whom this book would never have been written. I thank Lil for her patience, understanding, wisdom, and great guidance every step of the way. As for Lauren Winner, editor extraordinaire, it was a pleasure and an honor to have her wise counsel and sustaining support as this book came to be.

Any work such as this is written across a lifetime, and surely a "great cloud of witnesses" appear when I attempt to name those whose lives and prayers have taught me how to pray. I thank my father and mother and my dear aunt, whose prayers have always carried me, and I thank the family and friends whose prayers have brought me to this day. And surely I must express gratitude to every writer who ever picked up a pen to write the words that have brought me to a life of prayer and kept me there. Their words reverberate on every page.

Most of all, I realize that my deepest thanks is for the humble band of the men and women of God in the old, red brick church on Jared Street, in a little town in western Pennsylvania, now a lifetime ago. They taught me to pray. They showed me the way.

Finally, to Asa, Judd and Katie, and Gideon, for love I could never deserve, for prayers that sustain me, for the beautiful lives you live to the glory of God.

Linda McCullough Moore is the author of a novel, *The Distance Between*, and a collection of linked stories, *This Road Will Take Us Closer to the Moon*, as well as hundreds of poems, essays, short stories, and reviews. Linda lives and writes in western Massachusetts and loves to hear from readers at www.lindamcculloughmoore.com.